The Free Bird Flies

"Live your life from love, not loss."

—PHILLIP DALE FIFE

The Free Bird Flies

Choosing Life After Loss

Bert Fife

Voyages Press, Inc.
BIG CANOE, GEORGIA

First printing 2010
Second printing 2010

ISBN 978-0-9769934-3-8
LCCN 2009941916

ATTENTION ASSOCIATIONS, ORGANIZATIONS, SCHOOLS, HOSPICE, AND FUNERAL HOMES: Contact Voyages Press, Inc. for quantity discounts on bulk purchases. Phone: 706-869-8999. www.thefreebirdflies.com

Note to Reader

While reading this book there may be times that are tough to endure. Just like life, there are lessons beyond pain. How many times do you unknowingly stop short when the solution may be close at hand? If you can push though those difficult times, when tempted to stop......
Please...keep reading!

All names and photos used in this manuscript are "with permission."

Contents

> *"I have absolutely no fear of death. From my near-death research and my personal experiences, death is, in my judgment, simply a transition into another kind of reality."*
> *—Dr. Raymond Moody*

> *"There are basically moments in which you're in touch with the meaning of life, when your relationship to the rest of the universe makes sense."—Barbara De'Angelis*

> *"I love to think of nature as an unlimited broadcasting station, through which God speaks to us every hour, if we will only tune in." —George Washington Carver*

> *"Death is nothing else but going home to God, the bond of love will be unbroken for all eternity."—Mother Teresa*

Prologue

It's the day every mother hopes never happens, the day her world is shattered. This is my story of days in hell and the moments of grace that helped me out. Some events I talk about may cause you to pause and reflect on your own beliefs about death, life, and love. You did not pick up this book because you won the lottery and need suggestions for ways to celebrate. No, you have either lost one of the most treasured people in your life or you are close to someone who has. I invite you to consider the possibility that there is more to life than we know and that grace is present in our darkest hours. There is life after death for everyone.

Maybe you've never lost a child. Perhaps you have lost a loved one who is deeply connected to your image of yourself. As you touch that part of you that feels the grief, you can spring from it with renewed hope.

Life can be messy. This is not "pie in the sky" preaching that promises freedom if you just think differently. No, this book is about real life experiences that have left a scar on some of us. It provides an opening to consider alternative ways of navigating the days of our human existence. Some of it is mystical; some of it is practical application to provide resources for personal choices that can help you address grief in a more empowered way.

Grief has the power to destroy our lives if we allow it. Despite relentless pain, I considered the challenge to address my feelings and accepted the vulnerability inherent in the process. When tragedy trespassed on my corner of the world I tried to stand firmly against being a victim. With shaky knees and unshakeable resolve, I knew in my heart I owed it to my child, my family, and myself to begin learning to address loss in a productive way.

We often see life from a limited perspective. We act from a level of comfort based on conclusions reached from the information we choose to see at the time. Einstein said, "We can never solve a problem at the level it was created."

I ask you to step out of limited thinking into the realm of greater awareness. You may pose new questions for yourself about your personal belief systems. At least you are stretching your growing muscles and taking action to walk around the gaping black hole created by loss.

Even if my discoveries do not ring true for you, by talking about this book with others, you are helping to address the challenge of remaining in a physical body, moving in a physical world, without the physical presence of someone you love so deeply. If you stay on the planet long enough, death of a loved one is inevitable. This message gives guidelines for learning compassion, an invitation to practice non judgment, and suggestions of helpful tips to support yourself and one another. May it also serve as an opportunity to expand your awareness of subtle and sometimes astonishing signs to continue to connect you with your loved one in a healthy, life-affirming way.

CHAPTER 1

Curious About Death

"I have absolutely no fear of death. From my near-death research and my personal experiences, death is, in my judgment, simply a transition into another kind of reality."
—DR. RAYMOND MOODY

Even as a young child, I was curious about death. At the age of eleven I discovered my father was fifty five years old. For me, the eldest of two girls, fifty five was ancient. I had sad thoughts about Daddy dying, leaving me, and what would happen to him afterward. The Baptist church I attended said you had to be "saved" to get into heaven. I interpreted my Sunday school lessons and our minister's sermons to mean you had to walk down the church aisle and profess your faith, go to church, and not commit sins like dancing and drinking. Well, I had never seen my Daddy take that walk.

My larger than life Daddy was well liked for his great sense of humor. Spending afternoons sitting outdoors in the gentle Southern climate, he often whistled and sang all sorts of songs, including but not limited to church hymns. When I was elected to the sweetheart courts in high school, the girls in the court were sometimes escorted and shared the first dance with their fathers. Dad absolutely loved showing off his dancing skills to the younger fathers who were still busy building careers and probably not too concerned about dancing. I knew he liked his cocktails, was a fabulous dancer, and while he made sure we attended church, he enjoyed spending weekends boating and fishing. Like most of us, I was full of questions about death and dying, but not many answers worked for me.

As I got older, reading stories of near death experiences from people around the world held a fascination for me, particularly books on the topic by Dr. Raymond Moody. I observed how similar the stories were. All were from unrelated people who had an out of body near death experience yet they returned to their body to live. They seemed to have in common an incredible lightness, great love, and a knowing that there is much more to the continuation of life than we imagine. It gave me comfort to view death as a transition more than a definitive ending of our lives.

When I was called to the bedside of my Daddy, who lived to be ninety, I had a loving experience that confirmed my faith in the possibility that there is more to life than we know; God does exist and grace is present in our darkest hours. Standing by his bed I witnessed Daddy moving in and out of consciousness, extremely restless, like an unexpectedly awakened cat that frighteningly looks around, then returns to his nap only to be uncomfortably nudged again. This seemed to go on for hours as he lay on his deathbed.

Watching my loving father in this state of restlessness I recalled a prior visit when I unexpectedly asked him if he ever had dreams about his mother, the grandmother we all adored. She made her transition when I, her namesake, was five years old. He said he had dreamed she was lying motionless on a cold slab. From that conversation I sensed that Daddy's fear of dying was showing up in his dreams. Neither of us spoke any further about it.

During that same visit Daddy announced he was going to be eighty nine years old in July. I told him that according to the education that he so well provided, he was actually going to be ninety, born in 1907 and we were well into 1997. I laughingly told him age is a state of mind and if he wanted to be another age I would go along. He pensively responded, "Do you know how old ninety is? Who the hell wants to be ninety?" Obviously being ninety was not something he wanted to do, hence the call to his bedside a few weeks before his ninetieth birthday.

We had not discussed any of the stories and books I had read about what happens when we die. The fear in his eyes spoke volumes about how terrified he was. I'm certain the picture he had in his head was one of hellfire and damnation. Somehow, as if led by a higher source, I held my hands over his head and said this prayer, " May you see the light and step into it, may you see your mother and know you are safe, and may your guardian angel take you by the hand and lead you home." At that instant he relaxed into a deep sleep. It was another twenty four hours before his breath left his body. I felt God's presence strongly during this process and was thankful for the peace evident on his face.

My Dad's brother Ben had made his transition thirty years earlier. His daughter Joy lived away and was unaware of my Dad's declining health. I called to give her the news. She gasped when I told her and then said, "This morning in meditation, I saw my Dad walk toward your Dad to meet him. As they walked away together I could hear whistling." Hearing that story affirmed for me that Dad's death was certainly as peaceful as it seemed.

I think you will agree that a peaceful death is what we want for ourselves and our loved ones, but only when we are old. All loss is challenging. However, we expect to live and leave this earth chronologically; grandparents, parents, and then followed by children. We are conditioned to make some kind of sense out of time. When dealing with loss, timelines are worthless.

∞

CHAPTER 2

The Song of Life

*"There are basically moments in which you're in touch
with the meaning of life, when your relationship to
the rest of the universe makes sense."*

—BARBARA DE'ANGELIS

I lazily stayed in bed one summer June morning in 2006, eyes closed and languidly enjoying the drowsy state between the worlds of awake and dreaming. The sweet morning song of the family of sparrows that had made their home in the walled courtyard just outside my upstairs bedroom caused me to smile.

Waking up to their enthusiastic chirping was a pleasure I didn't allow myself until two and a half years ago when I sold my in-store marketing company. For eighteen years I had developed and nurtured a business that, while financially successful, demanded much of my time. As an entrepreneur raising five children, you may accurately assume I hit the ground running every morning.

As I listened to the chirping birds, I could hear individual notes blending together into one harmonious stream of sound. It reminded me of how we humans sing the individual song of our respective souls in our everyday existence. "What a treat, I love this," I thought, as I opened my eyes to a new day. I took a moment to simply appreciate myself. Slowing down, I could stop and smell the roses. I chose time with my children and friends, over frantic business endeavors.

Returning to the classroom for two business designations, Human Behavior Consultant and Certified Hypnotherapist, renewed my interest in helping others succeed. Individual coaching with young adults trying to find their place in the workforce, speaking to groups to help build better relationships, and working with non profits was my passion. This slower pace was delightful and the results seemed rewarding for both the teacher and the students. As the events of the month unfolded, I was ever more grateful for having changed the frantic work pace. It was more of a gift to me and my family than I could ever have imagined.

The sounds of the sparrow family led me to thoughts of my own family, my five grown children who ranged in age from 19 to 35. Their 'songs' were so alike, and yet so different, and I loved nothing more than being able to spend more time with them. The two oldest girls, Jamie and Stephanie, were married with children busy building their own family traditions. The younger three, Vivienne, Phillip and Tyler, were in various stages of finding their respective ways. I have always admired the healthy respect they have for one another.

The three youngest still required a little more parenting at this stage of our lives. Our twenty three year old, Vivienne, had graduated Louisiana State University and was working as administrative assistant to a well known international jewelry designer in NYC. Vivienne was the child I knew would succeed in whatever she decided. From the time of her birth she was dominant, direct, driven, demanding and totally "results oriented." When she was five she noticed a garage sale going on in our neighborhood. She came home, got her table from her play set and sold her brothers toys and a few clothes she found in my room. She would recruit the shoppers, show them her goods and ask them to pay whatever they wanted. She made ten dollars in a short time until her brothers' protests halted the venture. Vivienne was pleased; she had made the money she wanted. Vivienne has always been delightful. She commanded respect from her two younger brothers and they would do things like move her into the dorm, under her supervision of course, pick her up at the airport, and loan her one of their cars when she came home to visit.

The next youngest child and first son, Phillip, loved people, sharing ideas with others, and taking things apart to see what made them work. As a small child, he knew things that he could only have known had he come to the planet with that knowledge. From the age of four, he could provide answers to multiplication problems before anyone in the family. When he started school, he became frustrated because he knew the answers to math questions but he did not know how he got them. Always brilliant beyond his years, Phillip was never interested in school, career, or most things about the future and grew increasingly frustrated as he got older.

Phillip was usually a steady, supportive, inspiring kind of guy. Always popular, he could be exuberantly outgoing or shy and reserved depending on the circumstance. For sure, he was people oriented, impulsive, interactive, interested and insightful. He seemed to have a sixth sense about most things and people. His personality style caused him to be hard on himself and easy on others. Despite the fact that he constantly had allergic breathing problems, sinus problems, and upper respiratory complications, he was always smiling. His big blue eyes, surrounded by dark circles, were always twinkling.

When he was twelve, he had a seizure while spending the night with a friend. We had a multitude of tests run, including a brain MRI which never produced a diagnosis. The day we went to hear the doctor's report of the results, I was very concerned about the outcome. We stopped at McDonald's for burgers, and we were both tense and quietly concerned.

While we were sitting in the parking lot with the windows rolled down listening to a relaxing tune on the radio, a small sparrow came and sat on my window frame not more than inches from my face. It looked me directly in the eye. As we sat in silence the sparrow walked around the hood got on Phillip's window frame and looked directly at him. We both then breathed a sigh of relief, confident the test results would be fine. This little winged messenger delivered a comforting and spiritual experience. It was not much to acknowledge with words, but was just something to experience in your heart, a moment of grace and loving presence. As expected, the doctor was unconcerned about the seizure and Phillip was not given medications or restrictions and, to our knowledge, never had another seizure.

With his dimpled cheeks, he was quite the ladies man. He only loved two women, Brandy, his girlfriend since the sixth grade with whom he shared an on again off again romance for nine years, and his mother. You may identify with this or not but when you have children, there sometimes seems to be one who knows you better or connects with you more than the others. It's not that you love them any more than the others, it's just that the relationship is a little different. Phillip and I seemed to have a knowledge about one another that wasn't evident with any of my other children. Once as I was working in the kitchen, I had a minor accident and thought, but did not say, "ouch." All of the older children were around me, yet only two and a half year old Phillip asked from the adjoining room "Are you Ok Mom?" I remember being surprised how he knew I had hurt myself when he could not see me. And I was always surprised at how connected we seemed to be. Seemingly without words or close proximity, we knew when the other was hurt. There may have been other moments with the other children, but I remember this one particular moment vividly.

In his senior year of high school, Phillip and his brother moved to a smaller school. At graduation, the valedictorian mentioned traits of his classmates and said, "Not everyone could be as mature as Phillip Fife." His sisters and I almost fell off our chairs. As Phillip had always had a fabulous sense of humor but often an immature hot temper, we had a hard time getting this picture of maturity. The principal in his address said, "I have only recently gotten to know Phillip, an outstanding young man and a shining example." The Phil we knew was mainly concerned about having fun with his friends and family, pushing limits, and trying to figure out a fast track filled with little effort to live his life. He had always wanted to be an engineer and clearly had the mind to achieve that, yet never could understand why he couldn't just hang out a sign and do it. Going to school was not his favorite thing to do. Enrolling in Junior

College kept us off his back. He hated it and seldom attended class. He and his brother Tyler had been close since Tyler came onto the planet so Phillip waited for college until Tyler could attend too. From the reports from campus, that year they had more fun than most people have in a lifetime, which of course had nothing to do with academics.

Three months after Hurricane Katrina hit the Gulf Coast resulting in unusually heavy traffic in cities further inland, I got a call from the boys. They lost the key to the car and called me to come get them from college on Thanksgiving evening. Even though the drive was long, I had a convertible, the weather was nice, and we had a great time together returning home that night. The holiday traffic forced me to drive the back roads. Listening to music and laughing each time we stopped at a traffic light as Tyler would stand in the back seat to stretch his long legs and arms. I was grateful for the opportunity to spend this unexpected time with them. What could have been a stressful imposition turned out to be delightfully full of fun and a great way to begin our Thanksgiving celebration.

At twenty, Phillip and a high school buddy decided to move to Sedona, Arizona, to apprentice with my friend, Dennis Andries. Dennis is a celebrated, highly sought after trail guide and author of numerous books about Sedona. I know Dennis to be an amazing spiritual growth guide as well. Phillip was delighted when Dennis invited him to apprentice with him. Sedona was named by USA Today as The Most Beautiful Place in America. For the first time since he was a small child, there was a glimmer in Phillip's eye much like when he was a small child at Disney World. You know the feeling of exhilaration when you've waited in a long line, it's almost your turn, and you eagerly anticipate the thrill of a new adventure?

My children's father, Pete, had initiated and nourished in the boys a love for birds, nature, and the environment from the time they were born. They loved knowing the names and habits of the various birds that flew onto the property surrounding their home. They often shared hunting trips where bird watching was more prevalent than actually hunting. Their return home would be filled with stories about the beauty and excitement of the first bird flights at sunrise.

The adventure in Sedona was a natural fit for Phillip and his friend Mark, who grew up with the same appreciation for nature. Phillip was so restless that he did not know what he wanted to do from day to day. He often discussed his indecisiveness with me. Despite this restlessness, he was fun to be around, so the trip to Sedona held great promise for these two young men. The morning he and Mark left they were apprehensive and excited when they stopped by my house to say goodbye.

A few hours after their arrival in Sedona, they received a call that one of their friends back home in Baton Rouge, La. had died from sleep apnea. They felt compelled to come home and comfort their friends and the young man's mother. I can only imagine their young minds filled with dreams of hiking and adventure being faced with the shocking reality that a peer had suddenly died.

When I attended the young man's funeral, I felt I was there to hug any grieving son who needed it. Like most, I am uncomfortable in that environment but felt compelled to go. My heart went out to the boy's mother. Losing her son was hard enough and seeing his friends suffering was surely painful for her as well. Phillip came to my house afterward to let me know that one of the young men so appreciated that hug and said he knew he would be alright when he felt it. He thanked me for being there even though I did not really know the family. I was blessed by the strength and courage of the boys who mourned the loss of a friend.

Rather than return to Sedona, Phillip said that he couldn't stand to be away from his brother and did not plan to leave again without him.

Red-headed Tyler is the baby of the family. He is cool and reserved, making decisions only after getting the facts and analyzing the situation. But he is not somber: A born comedian, his dry wit can catch you off guard.

I received a message on my cell phone in "rapper" language which I assumed was from Phillip. I left him one in return with the same rap beat and different colorful words. A few hours later, Phillip came in the door laughing. He asked, "Are you planning to lay down some tracks for your new rapper career?" Tyler walked in the back door singing the rap. Apparently, I had the wrong son pegged for that clever song. Parenting these guys was full of surprises.

Tyler's versatile nature balanced Phillip's and Jamie's impulsiveness, Vivienne's driven high achieving nature, and Stephanie's cautious and careful side. Despite a twelve year difference in age, Tyler and Stephanie were always close, as Jamie and Phil were, in spite of a fourteen year difference. Somehow, in spite of each having completely unique personalities, they seemed to appreciate each other.

The strongest bond of all was between Tyler and his brother. While they scuffled as small boys, as teens and adults they were the best of friends. They shared friends, clothes, and adventures. No one could come between them, but their friendship instead drew many to them. Their parties, often held at my home without my knowledge, made them local legends and were always well attended. So it wasn't surprising that after graduating from high school, Tyler headed off to college with his big brother. They shared an apartment and the same schedule which allowed alternate class attendance. College was more about the social experience than the academic results for this dynamic duo.

∞

Their father and I divorced when the youngest were 10, 12, and 14. Vivienne lived with me after that and the boys with their father or me whenever they chose. It may seem an oxymoron, but it truly was a friendly divorce. Occasionally we still did things as a family and everyone seemed happy with the arrangement.

Most parents know how hard it is to stay connected to teenagers and young adults. Teens' busy lives along with the parent's many roles in the home and community often make it nearly impossible to keep up with it all. In 1999, I announced that we would have dinner together every Sunday, which began a tradition that continued for many years. The rules were if you were late, you didn't eat; if you did not come at all, you did not get an allowance. With this motley crew, it was always interesting to sit around a table and listen to their weekly stories. We all knew that Phillip would be the one who was late or a no show. The rest had the predictive personalities to be punctual. It did not take long for Phillip to understand he was going to be short of money during the week if he did not make the effort to attend family dinner. Although he occasionally skipped out for reasons we never discussed, as he matured he attended regularly, sharing the good times they all enjoyed. Jamie lived out of state so she and I would talk on Monday to catch up on news from Sunday's gathering. As they have gotten older, those are some of our fondest memories. It was one of my best efforts to keep them close and informed. I didn't have to ask many questions to get them to talk as they were eager to share their lives with their siblings as if I weren't there. During this time if I just sat silently I could learn so much about what was important to them.

Jamie lived out of state when she gave birth to her two girls. Although the younger ones had nieces, they didn't know much about the pregnancy process. Stephanie was here every Sunday during her pregnancy. It was amusing to hear the questions asked and the honest discussions about the experience of being pregnant.

When Treg, Stephanie's first son, was born, I left to get some food. When I came back the crib was empty so I assumed Treg was in the hospital nursery. When I moved toward Stephanie to deliver the food I then discovered Phillip holding him in a far corner. Tyler was standing beside him looking in wide eyed wonder at their brand new nephew. I will always remember the pride of that loving moment as Stephanie shared her first born with her brothers in such a trusting way. The boys seemed to already feel a relationship with their nephew. Stephanie and her husband Benji had shared their anticipation with them before his birth during our Sunday gatherings.

∞

Raised in a Christian home, my children attended a Catholic church and school. Growing up Baptist, I converted to Catholicism when their father and I married. I always thought it important to give children a good faith foundation on which to begin finding their own answers to the inevitable questions posed by life.

To me, dogma is not as important as the willingness to have a relationship with a loving God. As a family, we rely on the strength, power and mystery of a God greater than anything we can conceive, and yet closer to us than our own heartbeat. There are many paths to one God. I always felt that God is an ever present energy force, never a judge; a loving presence within our own being. It is difficult for me to see God as an outside entity making lists and decisions based on our behavior when we've been given the gift of free will.

As part of something wise and balanced, I believe we have an inner knowledge that can be accessed if we can be still long enough to listen. Have you ever had a "gut feeling" or just felt something was going to happen? Maybe someone calls on the phone at the time you are getting ready to call them. To me that is intuition, something we all have, acknowledged more by some than others. It is an important part of our being that can be sharpened if it is our intention to do so.

I have always felt a sense of Angelic or Spiritual presence, more an intuitive feeling than anything else. There is something larger than our physical selves. There were times in my life that the only explanation for safety or survival was an Angelic intervention. We can develop our intuitive nature and connection to Divine guidance through prayer and meditation. My faith in Divine help is strong and I know that prayer is answered, not always in the way I want with my limited human understanding, but always answered.

When Tyler was six weeks old, Pete and I went out for dinner while sixteen year old Jamie kept the baby. When we returned we found that she had slipped on the wooden floor and dropped him. His eyes were fixed and unchanging so we immediately rushed him to the emergency room. He was diagnosed with a skull fracture and a pediatric neurologist was called in who recommended an overnight hospital stay for observation. He would probably be fine, but needed to be monitored. Due to the swelling, Tyler's head was misshapen and we were told it would remain that way for at least six weeks.

I didn't see his x-ray that night, which was so unlike me. With a degree in health sciences, I knew how to read them and always insisted on seeing them the few times we suffered those small accidents inevitable when raising children. As I held Tyler to my heart, I prayed to God unceasingly. A strong sense said that I needed to take him home and watch over him. It was one of those moments when what you are thinking may not make sense to others, but it does to you.

Against the doctor's recommendation, we went home with him and I sat by his bedside throughout the night. Once again, led by a Higher Power felt deeply within my soul, I confidently placed my hands around his head and prayed that he be healed, whole, and healthy.

The next night was Jamie's sixteenth birthday party at our home. It was important to continue with the birthday plans so Jamie could begin to overcome her scare. As over sixty-five teenagers partied loudly on our outdoor patio, Pete and I held vigil over the bassinette which held our precious six week old. By the end of the night, Tyler's head was shaped perfectly and he was acting and appearing perfectly well and normal. It truly was a happy birthday for Jamie and the proud parents.

A few days later we returned to the doctor for our follow-up appointment. While waiting for the Doctor to come into the room, I glanced at the x-ray hanging on the light. What I saw frightened the breath out of me. There was a large gap of separation of the skull bone creating a semi-circle of trauma around his little head. Thankfully, I had not seen this the night of the fall. I might not have had the faith or strength to pray and affirm perfect health for Tyler that night.

God works in wonderful ways that we do not understand. That day, I was so thankful for answered prayer, and the strength to believe without seeing. He might have done just fine in the hospital. I believe my God sent Holy Helpers for our family to remind me of my ability to hold strong to my faith in things I couldn't understand, yet only needed to believe. Tyler's perfect health was confirmed by the physician. We returned home, amazed once again how life changes in a moment.

I taught the children about living with more than our five senses and to trust their gut feelings or inner wisdom. They believed that Jesus' most important lesson was to love, and that Christian meant aspiring to practice "Christ-like" qualities. We lived with gratitude for all God's blessings because the spirit of God in all of us wants only our highest good.

One loving gift from our chosen God is free will. It just never felt right to me that God would tell us how to live, only to punish us if we chose to do it the hard way. I know in my heart that God loves us whether we love God or not. If we pay attention there is a plan for our highest good. Nothing ever happens by accident as our lives unfold to fulfill our Divine purpose. It is less important how long it takes us to understand the lessons, than for us to know how rich our learning will be when we love one another and ourselves through it all.

My children know about their personal responsibility for staying close to their Divine path. If they choose thoughts and actions that create detours off the path, then there are consequences; but these consequences can serve to strengthen their faith. Events may happen to provide an opportunity to birth a new awareness in ourselves and a chance to examine the way we respond.

We live with the knowledge that we are spiritual beings having a human existence to integrate our Divinity and humanity. Things happen we can't explain, yet we must accept them as part of our human experience for the growth of our souls.

This teaching was once exemplified for the boys when they attempted to celebrate Tyler's graduation from high school in Donaldsonville, Louisiana. After the ceremony, we told Phillip he was in charge of his brother's safety that night and to be sure he safely enjoyed himself. Bluntly, he was the designated driver if necessary. Two months before, his Dad called to discuss our invitation to join other families in a group graduation party allowing twenty five guests per student for a fixed fee. When we asked Tyler, he didn't have much information about it and seemed uninterested. We decided not to plan on participation. Our fifth child's high school graduation was considered overkill for the "must attend" events for our families. In short, we would have a hard time getting twenty five people to celebrate with. A young man in the graduating class invited Tyler and Phillip to be two of his twenty five paid guests. It was understood they would leave the church together and go to the reception hall.

I was awakened by a call from Phillip saying Tyler had been asked by one of the mothers in charge to leave the party because he hadn't paid his fee. They were having such a good time that Phillip asked her to let him stay. He tried to explain that the friend had already paid for him, then offered to give her the amount of money she requested. The mother in charge insisted he leave citing a decision made prior to the event by the party committee. Quite upset and not understanding such rude adult behavior, Phillip called me to discuss it. I recommended he bring Tyler to Baton Rouge, where other friends were having parties. They had friends graduating from schools all over town. Little did we know how different the night would unfold.

Two hours later, another call from Phillip reminded me of something I taught them that seemed to be true. As a mother it was one of those times when I felt I had done something right. As they left the party, they got a call from their friend, Charlie. He returned from college the week of graduation to learn his mother was dying from a rare lung disorder. Charlie had attended grade school, played basketball in our driveway and on the school court with the boys. Phil and Tyler hadn't seen him in a while since he had chosen to go away to school. Charlie called Phillip for comfort when he heard the news about his mother.

Phillip knew they would have missed the distressing call from Charlie if that angry and irritated mother at the graduation had not insisted they leave. The sadness of a friend about to lose his mother would not have been heard.

After receiving that call, he and Tyler went to Charlie's and spent the night sitting on his front porch giving the comfort and support Charlie needed to help him deal with this heartbreaking reality. Phillip called me to express his awe relative to the events of the night. Considering how important this seemed to each of them, suddenly it all made sense. The next afternoon when I spoke to Tyler to see how he felt about missing his graduation celebration, he said he would not have missed watching the sun come up with Charlie and Phillip that morning. I was never more proud of those three boys who could reach out to one another for support, despite outer circumstances, and unite their hearts in wonder and sorrow. That was such a spiritual moment for them all and one which I felt blessed to have been told about.

Often the people who irritate you the most can be your best teachers on this journey we call life. My thanks to the "mean" mother who unknowingly took part in such a blessed opportunity for learning. For the boys, it was another one of those "Grace Moments" when Divine Wisdom meets human experience. Can you remember a time when you just knew something larger than you had happened?

A young man of courage and strength, Charlie, since losing his mother, is in law school and has a bright future filled with loving possibilities. He is an inspiration as he continues to choose life after loss.

Life as we knew it was wonderfully blessed with a loving environment to grow and play in. Seemingly, all was well in our world.

∞

CHAPTER 3

The Free Bird Flies

"I love to think of nature as an unlimited broadcasting station, through which God speaks to us every hour, if we will only tune in."
—GEORGE WASHINGTON CARVER

On a beautiful summer day, I stepped into my walled courtyard to go to my garage when I noticed a baby sparrow sitting on the back of my outdoor chair. After close observation, it became apparent that the other birds had flown away. He was not ready to clear the height and was left behind. He looked nervously apprehensive and unsure how to fly freely. Stopping to look into his eyes, I reminded him that he could be free when he was strong enough to flap his wings and fly away. I looked at that bird so lovingly and felt an inexplicably strong connection to its life.

Returning home to find the baby bird was still there, I once again reminded him of his choice and intention which could lead to his impending flight. For three days, I encouraged the little growing sparrow that looked so desperate to be free. After all, free birds always fly away.

On the third day, I returned to discover that instinctively the little bird had indeed flown. He no longer needed my encouragement and was finally really free to discover a new world just for him. Had those three days seemed long to him? Where would he go? I thought of the words of the old gospel song I'd heard my father sing, "His Eye is On the Sparrow and I know He Watches Me."

Although I knew his flight was inevitable, and completely natural, a deep sadness swept over me. He flew freely on his terms, not mine. I never knew when or if I would see him again. Weeks later I realized the significance of this encounter.

∞

CHAPTER 4

The Day the Birds Stopped Singing

*"Death is nothing else but going home to God,
the bond of love will be unbroken for all eternity."*
—MOTHER TERESA

The morning of July 22, 2006, I awakened with a feeling unlike any I had ever known. My heart was aching so deeply. It seemed like it would never stop. I did a mental check: the boys were home with friends, Vivienne in NYC, Stephanie and her family was in Florida on vacation, and Jamie and her family had just moved from Massachusetts to Ohio due to her husband's job transfer. Things seemed fine, yet the aching was still present. My friend Donald was helping me prepare for our friend Patti's birthday celebration that night at my home. I shared my heavy heart with him and he advised that I just stop and cry if I felt like it. It felt so confusing to have these outbursts of agony amidst cleaning, cooking, and preparing for a party. I couldn't figure out why I felt such deep sadness like never before. I would literally burst into tears, wail with deep sorrow, dry my eyes and continue my work.

Around noon Phillip called to tell me Tyler had to work and Stephanie's family was out of town, so he and I were the only two family members available to attend our routine Sunday lunches. He suggested that we go to a restaurant together so I would not have to cook and clean. I thanked him for attending a community play with me the night before where we left one another smiling and teasing who was going to call who first. At this time on Saturday, he and his friend Mark were in the car together laughingly trying to figure out how they were going to rid their father's property of the smell left from a wild boar. A group of friends showed up from a hunting outing, promptly dressed it on the premises and were now concerned about clean up. Each time I thought I had heard it all; something like this pig adventure would catch me by surprise. Never a dull moment as each activity was undertaken with such enthusiasm. One thing I knew for sure was that Phillip could gag when looking at leftover table food, so this pig story made me chuckle. We agreed to talk after church the next day to choose our restaurant.

The evening started with my guest's arrival for the dinner party to honor Patti's birthday. Her father was in attendance which was particularly delightful since her mother had passed away earlier and it was a sweet time to spend with her aging father. Another couple, Melinda and John, attended as well. Melinda, a professional voice talent, is often contracted to be the spokesperson or radio voice for multiple commercials. That night I had the radio on, something I have never done for a party. I usually play CD's of soft music but somehow it was the radio that night. The Lady of the Lake Hospital had a commercial by Melinda and the radio station played it an inordinate number of times during our gathering. We all commented on the multiple replays wondering why that unusual occurrence was actually happening. Although a birthday celebration is always a motivation for me to surround myself with friends and honor the birthday, that night things seemed surreal.

At 12:30 AM, after the guests had left, Tyler called and said a friend of ours with the local police department knocked on his door and said Phillip was at St. Elizabeth's Hospital, he had been in an accident. Tyler had gone to St. Elizabeth's and was told he was at Our Lady of the Lake Hospital twenty five miles away and closer to my home. Was this the reason for the commercial we kept hearing over and over? Had I been gently warned to pay attention? When I called the emergency room they said there was no patient there by my son's name. I calmly got dressed to go and see for myself. Raising two boys brought unplanned trips to the hospital to handle minor injuries so I expected that once again there may be a broken arm or some minor scratches. As I walked toward the door of the emergency room, a paramedic was wiping things down from the ambulance. When I stopped to inquire about Phillip she asked me if I was his mother and quickly directed me inside.

I was met by a chaplain who spoke little English and seemed to be at a loss for words in any language. It still did not dawn on me that things were serious until he tried to lead me into a smaller more intimate waiting room. When I said I would rather sit in the larger room, he insisted I go into the smaller. As my friend Donald parked the car, I was followed into the small room by the ambulance driver who offered to pray with me. The prayer request was that Phillip would not suffer. I knew it was more serious than I could conceive. Donald, Tyler, his friend Jared, and I were in the room when the doctor uttered the statement that would change our lives forever: "I'm sorry, we did everything we could." When asked if I would like to see him, I knew for me it would not be necessary. Tyler said he felt the same. We always wanted to remember him vibrantly alive. Sitting in that room after the news, a clerical employee entered with a portable computer informing us of the hospital room that was being assigned to Phillip. My grief filled eyes brightened as I realized there was some mistake, he was really alive. As she proceeded to talk, Donald informed her of the news we had just received. I watched my hopes die when she repeatedly apologized for her error. Never before have I so desperately wanted something to be a lie. I begged them to just tell me it wasn't so.

Calling his father to come home from San Diego, where he and his wife Sharon were attending a conference, I dialed the number, started to speak but no sound would come out of my mouth. I was numb and seemingly unable to say the words. Donald retrieved the phone, took a deep breath, and told Pete the alarming news. Phillip's father was delayed in San Diego and could not get a flight home. His delay lasted two days which was probably hell on earth for him and his loving wife Sharon. The call no parent wants had come like a thief in the night to rob us of our sense of how the world should be.

∞

For some of you, not seeing your child after an accident would be unthinkable. Others may agree with my decision. I am innately visual and try to be careful what pictures I see. Phillip's face the night before when he and I parted was the memory I wanted to remain untarnished. Whenever faced with life's tough decisions one must only do what is best for them and allow others to do the same.

Many times this is when relationships are bruised and some are never restored because of harsh judgments made during a most trying time of life. If you've lost a child or someone dear to you, it is most helpful to take care of yourself and not punish others with your version of how they should or should not act, what they say or not say, what they feel or not feel. Grief is one of life's most personal experiences and should be honored as such. It can destroy the healthiest of relationships if you let it.

For the next few months I moved out of numbness into acknowledgment and back into numbness. I had shared my body's sustenance with this child, and a part of me had seemingly died. The numbness allowed my body to take care of itself in a more gentle way.

∞

Do you believe in God? Do you believe in anything? Do you even know what you believe? Answering these questions would take effort and attention.

Losing my first born son at twenty-one, just as we had glimpsed at one another through mutually adult eyes, shook every cell in my being. I still sometimes feel that shake on the inside and maybe I always will. His free spirit and sense of adventure caused Phillip many close calls during his short lifetime, yet I certainly never thought I would outlive him. It seems that this night my son, the best driver I knew, hit a concrete culvert at 70 MPH on his way home. Of course there were many questions. How could such a great driver be killed in a lone accident just a few miles from home? Was alcohol or drugs involved? Where was he before this tragedy?

Over time these questions were answered by the unknowing human spiritual messengers who appeared at the most unusual times when I could appreciate the message. At the funeral home where people stood waiting in line for more than an hour to offer their condolences, a woman appeared and told us that she was the first emergency responder who worked on our son. She said that she may be prohibited from visiting in these situations but felt compelled to come meet us and comfort us in any way possible. I asked her if she thought alcohol was a factor and she said definitely not because she was in his face for quite some time and did not suspect alcohol to be a factor. She stated she had lots of experience with alcohol-related accidents. She was convinced it was not in this case. I knew she had been sent by God to answer that question. Maybe in some mysterious way Phillip had encouraged her too.

Phillip wasn't feeling well the Saturday before the accident and, like most twenty one year old young men, did not tell me, his mother. The night of the accident, apparently, he was going to a friend's house and had stopped to check on his beloved grandmother who lived next door to him. His father was out of town so Phillip adopted the caring of his Grandmother whom he adored. His grandfather had passed away nine years prior. He told his Granny she could feel safe because he often drove through her circular driveway to check on things before going home. He asked if she wanted him to spend the night and she said that would not be necessary and told him to go out and have fun with his friends because she felt safe. He said he didn't feel very well but like most young people, went anyway.

The boys at the party said afterward that Phillip did not have anything to drink that night. He stayed at the party less than an hour, saying he felt badly, he began his twenty five mile journey home. After calling to check in with Tyler, he only made it twenty of those miles. With no skid marks on the road or any evidence of duress he slammed into that fatal culvert. The boy hosting the party that night was a long-time friend. He said Phillip was acting strangely the way he did the night he had the seizure and he was convinced that he had another seizure, which caused the accident. There was no need for an autopsy due to the amount of trauma, so the seizure was never medically confirmed. In my heart I knew it was true.

Death always occurs when the soul has done its earthly mission, but when it's your child, your beloved, you want some answers, some comfort, something to begin to heal this gaping hole in your heart. My free bird had flown.

It is amazing how our human minds and bodies respond to such shocking loss. When Tyler and I returned home from the hospital, we sat on the sofa, looked at one another and said we were tired and wanted to go to sleep. Surprisingly, we both said good night, went to our respective beds, as if we could wake up to discover it was all a nightmare. Jared was with us and apparently had called others. When I got up minutes later, my home and driveway was filled with young men and women crying their hearts out, some screaming at God, other's with their heads down, unable to move. From that moment, I knew this loss would shake the faith, the core, and the future of us all. As we all tried to make sense of a seemingly senseless happening, we walked around aimlessly. I had given permission for donation of Phillip's organs and at three thirty in the morning received a phone call from the organ donation staff telling me that there was not enough fluid left in them for harvesting. I felt that this was cruel and unusual punishment for a mother who had only earlier been given such tragic news. Maybe they should rethink this process to show more compassion. We definitely wanted to make a difference in the lives of some other persons if possible. However, after the dreadful news I had just received, this information could have waited.

∞

At my request, that window to the courtyard from my upstairs bedroom had been covered with black fabric to block out all light. From my bed on that painful Sunday morning, I picked up the phone and told Phillip's sisters the news about their brother. I will always remember those gut wrenching soul shaking phone conversations when the veil of innocence we so try to preserve for our children was violently pierced. I knew the long trip back to Baton Rouge that Phil's siblings had to take, from Ohio, New York, and Florida would be filled with hours of memories and heartfelt tears for their loss. As for me, I could not get out of my bed for the weight of the world held me down. Thankfully, I was now surrounded by friends who would begin to help me learn to breathe again. Nina, my longstanding friend who had lost a son at nine months, came from out of town. While other dear friends and my sister came to help, having someone there who knew what it was like to lose a child became a tremendous source of comfort for me. Together they handled details like writing an obituary, keeping the food moving, and what seemed like a million phone calls. As I was paralyzed with grief, others were able to move. I did not care about anything at this point. All I wanted was to hug Phillip again.

Through the social rituals we have come to expect when someone dies, decisions about caskets, open or closed, cremations, programming, participants, all details which are so overwhelming, we somehow move about in slow motion, numb to the experience. We then realize the result of these actions by either us or someone else is that the life of our beloved has been summarized and packed away. The pain has only begun. You must now begin to choose what to do about your daily life.

Having nowhere to be or a schedule to follow, provided time for me to lie in my darkened room and feel the pain at a time I did not want to feel better. I knew the truth about death's transition, but I needed to grieve, to honor the earthly life of Phillip Fife, my firstborn son. In retrospect it might have been better had I gone to a workplace, spent time with others, and had something to focus on. However, when death presents itself, we do the best we can with what we know and have.

Time cannot be measured for grief. It is a moment to moment process. I am occasionally late for appointments and have always said that we live on God's time. We made up time as we know it. Before this event I had little attachment to time, and I really do not have any attachment now. Twenty one years may be a nanosecond on God's clock and ninety years a whole second. Why should I time my grief? I can only experience it in the way that works for me; forget time.

Light is symbolic of clarity of vision in seeing what is. It is no wonder that I wanted the blinds drawn and to put my head under the covers. To step into the light meant I would be forced to see the truth. There was an accident. I would no longer answer phone calls from Phillip about something funny that happened. He would not be sitting in his chair at Sunday dinners. I did not want to be enlightened.

∞

CHAPTER 5

Searching for Wings

"When we walk to the edge of all the light we have and are about to step out into the darkness of the unknown, we must believe that one of two things will happen. We will find solid ground to stand on, or God will teach us to fly."
—AUTHOR UNKNOWN

A few weeks after my life altering experience, I received a call from a young man I had met only months before. His excitement was evident as he shared the story of a job offer he'd received, the very job he was well groomed for, and his story of almost losing his faith while waiting for his big opportunity. Earlier I had shared with him the above quote from an unknown author, words that kept him going amidst his doubts.

I told him about my loss. He immediately apologized for his poor timing; however, I knew that God was speaking through him directly to me. I needed to be reminded of those words and how I too could find solid ground or wings. Chris must have heard the glimmer of hope in my voice that I might have a purpose for life when I advised him of his next steps toward getting his dream job. I needed him as much as he needed me. Together we both grew that week in unexpected loving ways. He got his job and I began to open the shades and come out from under the covers.

In earlier times, when a death occurred, we wore black for a period to signal the community we were in mourning. That might still be a good idea. Until now, I was usually the one smiling and saying positive things, unaware of the compassion that some people needed. Many times I am sure, when I unknowingly encountered someone who may have been grieving; it did not occur to me how deep their pain might be. What a lesson when I went to the store and the checkout person smiled and asked how I was. For once in my life, I could not fake it. I wanted to scream, "My son is dead! How do you think I am?" Instead, I lowered my head and said nothing.

Another day, a young man who reminded me of Phillip came to stand next to me in the bank line. In the middle of my transaction, my brain thought how unfair it was that my son wouldn't be able to start a business, have a bank account, or experience a young family. I stood at the counter sobbing uncontrollably.

As a society we are so uncomfortable with grief, possibly because we often "play pretty" and hide our pain. Some postulate that the reason we are so uncomfortable is that we live in an instant world, instant food, instant drinks, and instant results when we push a button. Grief is not an instant event. It is a process that takes as long as it takes. To their credit, while the bankers were uncomfortable, they reached out by listening with compassion, allowing me to express my heartfelt grief and disappointment that my dreams for my son would not be realized.

Early in my grief I found that I feared I would begin to cry and not be able to stop. Over time, I was less uncomfortable crying in public because I eventually learned that I could stop. When others are not comfortable with your grief, as with most things people say or do, it is not personal. Often, in discussions with people I may get tears in my eyes. When my heart is full, my eyes may leak. Others' reaction is to think they have caused the crying and immediately apologize. Talking is helpful and it is even more helpful when people can be comfortable with my tears, to allow me to feel without feeling responsible for the cause.

∞

For years I did not have time to watch television and really didn't miss it thinking it was a mindless way to spend my life. At this point in my grief, mindless activities worked for me twenty four hours a day. I discovered that sometimes with love and compassion, God sends messages even through mindless television viewing. A man named John Diaz was on The Oprah Show talking about surviving a plane crash. As he escaped from the front of the plane he watched as passengers in the center of the plane burst into flames to their death.

While that was certainly a tragic event, I was relieved to know that he had seen what he referred to as an "aura" of light around them as their spirits left their bodies. He said some were brighter than others. His lesson through this was to live his life so that when he exits this earth his light will be bright. This supported my belief that we only change forms when we exit this earth. The part of us that's real, our spirit, lives forever. I also believe that whether the light is bright or dark, we go to a place of unimaginable love and peace whenever we leave the earth. I was thankful for Mr. Diaz's life affirming appearance on a day when I was wrestling with doubt.

There were a few moments in those first few months that brought me a glimmer of hope in despair. Another television show was about mothers in Africa, dying of AIDS, holding little babies in their arms who were trying to nurse with no chance of getting the nutrients they needed to survive. After losing Phillip I constantly asked, "Why me?" Asking "why" was a mantra I had adopted. There was a brief moment of clarity when I saw these suffering mothers. Why not me? Did I think I was somehow special? Did I think that I was better than this poor mother who was watching her child die due to no fault of her own? Her body was unable to support her child's life, so she watched helplessly as her baby died in her arms.

I felt arrogant and selfish at the thought of being superior to this mother. Sharing her story created a shift in my thought patterns to either change the question or stop questioning at all. Since I was so exhausted from suffering, I was about to stop questioning, when it occurred to me to ask, "What am I going to do now?" It was a shift in consciousness that stopped giving the power to something outside myself and returned it to me. I realized I alone could begin to consider that question. I will answer that question daily for the rest of my life. Somewhere within those spinning questions, I heard my son's voice say to me, "Live your life from love, not loss." This was a tall order for a suffering mother.

The question that loomed in my mind from the moment I received the news was, "How can I ever get over this?" On one of the many days when I felt like a victim, a phone call came from Dr. Lusco, my friend and the doctor who delivered my children. He was out of the country at the time of Phillip's accident, returning to this tragic news.

Tyler was born the same year I began my business. Dr. Lusco reminded me that arriving for my appointments, like most working mothers, I had two toddlers under five, a "to-do" list as long as my arm and the requisite "can do" attitude. His call to express his sadness and concern included saying the magic word that jump-started my relationship with grief. Until this point I couldn't comprehend how I would ever get over losing Phillip. Dr. Lusco's words sound simple yet they were like a lifeline to me. He said, "I remember how you successfully managed your business and those children. You will now do what you do best. Manage your grief." Hope was born in my heart that day. Despite the messages from my spiritual helpers, hope was absent until I heard that word, a word I could understand: *Manage* your grief. We manage our lives from moment to moment by the words we speak and the actions we take. I was so tired of thinking I would never get over it. Now, I would begin to *manage* it.

∞

CHAPTER 6

Exploring Depth

"It is not the length of life, but depth of life."
—RALPH WALDO EMERSON

My years of studying and reading about death may help me on this journey but in no way prepared me for it. Losing my son is the most painful and heart wrenching event my human existence can imagine. Life continues despite our human suffering because it is deeper than we imagine.

Immediately following the news, nothing seems helpful. You only know that you are frighteningly vulnerable. There are few rules for how you can handle this. You should not break any laws, even if you feel like it. Other than that it's a "make it up as you go" process that feels right for you.

In her book, Where Angels Walk, Joan Wester Andersen's son was returning from college in a life threatening snow storm when he encountered a tow truck driver who brought him home safely. The next morning there was no evidence that the truck ever existed. Her son relayed the story about how the driver approached the side of the vehicle without any sign of ever driving into view, offered help, then seemed to disappear immediately after their arrival. No charge, no contact information. Their family suspected it was an angel. In her quest for more evidence of surreal experiences she placed ads in publications to ask others for their stories. To her surprise, her mailbox was stuffed with story after story about angelic intervention. When I read this book years ago, I felt like some of my beliefs had been affirmed. Perhaps I was not crazy to believe in divine help.

I discussed some of the stories with many people who had a look of recognition. They began to tell their stories of transformation after tragedy. Many shared stories about their loved ones coming to them in some way to let them know they were alright. It is helpful to hear others' stories of life affirming communication from unexpected sources. Throughout this book I share some of these with you. I continue to be encouraged when impromptu discussions spring up among anxious people who are eager to tell what happened; yet afraid someone might think them strange. Comfort comes from knowing we are not alone.

I refer to the messengers from heaven, or the other side, as Guides and sometimes Angels. I only know that they are from a loving God energy who wants our highest and best for our soul's journey. Some helpers are loved ones who have crossed over to the other side of the thin veil that separates us.

We are spiritual beings having a human experience. You may wonder why some people seem to be "spared" death and others experience the seeming finality of death. I have come to believe that it's all part of life. We only know it from our limited human existence.

The life experience includes physical death, not a spiritual death. We live on in another existence according to our soul's journey to move closer to perfection and God. From now on I refer to Phillip's exit from the earth plane as a transition or a crossing over as I have come to understand it. Staying on this planet is impossible for the free bird whose soul is ready to fly. The method of exit is inconsequential to the other side.

In my early studies of near death, it seemed that in a violent death where the body may be severely injured, there would be only violence on this side. Of the people who had out of body experiences and who later returned, the pain was absent as long as they were out of body. You may wonder, "Why would they have to come back if it is so painful?" They knew they had to return to the physical because their soul's purpose had not been completed. The pain only became present when their souls were reunited with their bodies to remain here on earth. Many of them described how they did not want to return and remembered vividly the pain they experienced the moment they did return. Apparently, the pain is only on this side of that thin veil, the side of the physical. This is important to us when we lose someone. We want to know they are okay. My experience from others' loss, as well as my own, shows me that when the transition is made, our loved one is fine no matter what their death experience. Their soul moves into another realm of existence. After the loss, I knew Phillip was fine. I just was not sure I could be.

∞

CHAPTER 7

Sister Ameline's Gift

"I believe there are two sides to the phenomenon known as death, this side where we live, and the other side where we shall continue to live. Eternity does not start with death. We are in eternity now."
—NORMAN VINCENT PEALE

A few weeks before Phillip's transition, Sr. Ameline, my children's pre-kindergarten teacher many years prior, called to announce her retirement and ultimate relocation to her hometown. She said she would like to see my children so we arranged a breakfast with the two boys. They loved Sister's classroom, the class's pet rabbit at Easter, Christmas plays where they played Joseph, and class trips to interesting places. Mostly they loved Sister's childlike spirit of wonder and connection to the outdoors. Living on two acres on a small river flowing through town, a few blocks from school, the children usually had friends over to play and loved being in the outdoors with the birds, turtles, and mud on rainy days. Sister Ameline would sometimes spend a holiday with us or come over for some outdoor adventure. To their Dad's delight, the boy's knowledge and appreciation for animals and birds grew as they got older. Sister always loved this and had known how excited they were about those things as little tykes in pre-kindergarten.

On this particular day, we had a grown-up breakfast while sharing stories about the boys' classroom adventures. Sister had a very good memory and could remember details of conversations and complaints of a four year old which happened fourteen years ago. We all loved that about her. When we arrived, the boys had each bought her a gift card to spend as she wished with notes thanking her for teaching. When she realized the gift cards could be used any way she chose, she announced that she intended to purchase Thomas Kinkade's print Stairway to Paradise. She thought that was her next preparation on her journey of life. Phillip said, "Sister, that is such a beautiful print." Ameline and I both looked at each other strangely and she asked him how he knew about it. His words were, "I am personally familiar with it." Phillip had never expressed an interest in art. Even though we looked at one another strangely neither of us questioned him further. I am not sure he consciously knew the importance at that time. We remember the conviction with which he spoke that day.

The day of Phillip's transition, Sister Ameline had just arrived in San Antonio, Texas for a long awaited, much anticipated meeting of the Sisterhood. When I called she insisted on returning to town. Thankfully, she followed her heart, because of her kindness and deeply felt love for Phillip, helped plan his funeral and led her to give a testament to his life at his service.

I was not sure I even wanted to have a traditional funeral service. Preferring the idea of cremation or scientific donation, I do not feel it is necessary to place a body in a box and put it in or above the ground. In my belief, the body is like a pair of favorite pajamas. When we make our transition, we drop our pajamas and the spiritual part of us that is real, lives on. However, Phillip's grandmother was Catholic and out of loving respect for her, I chose to do the traditional closed casket and Catholic mass. Phillip attended Catholic school and sometimes went to mass as an adult, so I knew for him it was appropriate as well.

During Sister Ameline's tribute to Phillip's life, she spoke of the Kinkade print Stairway to Paradise and the conversation with him about it just a couple of weeks before. A woman who sold the print was in attendance, went home, and came back with a framed print. Apparently, two weeks earlier she felt strongly that she needed to order the print.

She seldom ordered anything like that unless someone had requested it with the intent to pay. This particular time she ordered it without question. Without hesitation or discussion, she delivered it to the funeral home where it was placed next to Phillip. It seemed so appropriate since it represented Sister Ameline's last visit with him. The beautiful print of a stairway, surrounded by colorful flowers and sunlight, suggestive of a crossing to a more peaceful place, stayed by his casket.

The funeral staff transferred the print along with the flowers to the church for the funeral service. After the service, it was returned to the funeral home along with hundreds of plants and flowers. The children and I stopped at the funeral home to gather plants and flowers for hospitals and nursing homes. Tyler's best friend, Jared, and Steve, Vivienne's boyfriend, placed the framed print in the locked trunk of Jared's car. Little did we imagine the mystical journey of that print now so famous within our family circle.

Early the next morning, Phillip's father called to relay what happened as he and Sharon were cleaning the house. He moved a chair, cleaned under it and moved it into the archway of the adjoining room. Moments later, Sharon came from the back of the house, stopped and asked him where he'd found the print which was propped-up in the chair he had just moved and cleaned under. Imagine his surprise to see it there, without explanation. We believe without a doubt that somehow Phillip or someone in the other realm materialized that picture to assure his father that he was ok. After all, he had apparently walked the stairway to paradise. Of the two people who knew where the print was, one was sleeping upstairs with the keys to the trunk and the other was at my home twenty miles away. Neither of them had any knowledge of the print's appearance and both were quite shocked by finding it. I only know that Phillip's father found great comfort in that mystical experience and was less concerned about how it happened and more thankful that it did. Later that picture was placed on a stand on the floor where the family Dachshund leaned against it and cried for hours. After being hung on the wall, a hawk (which later proved to be providential) came each morning to look at it.

Somehow that picture symbolized Phillip's journey into the unknown. According to Kinkade, it was Paradise.

Months later, Sister Ameline took a photo of her new Kinkade print. In the photo was an unexpected bright shining orb, which we now suspect was a symbol of Phillip's presence. Making a special trip to show me the orb, she explained that it was definitely not a light reflection because she made sure there was no light to reflect. She has since moved to her hometown and planted a tree for Phillip which is growing beautifully. What a gift she provided by introducing that print to us at the perfect time. I am sure he watches over her and communes with her due to their strong connection on the earth path.

∞

I had gone to visit Phillip's grandmother and for the first time since his transition, had a chance to speak with her alone. As we talked, tears began to flow down her face as she said how much she missed Phillip, who she always referred to as "my boy." The love I felt from her was overwhelming, as if she and Phillip's combined love was coming through her at that moment. I thought at the time that she would soon be with him. Her health had begun to fail and her grief was evident. December 30, 2008 at the age of 92, his beloved grandmother made her transition to be with him.

After her death, Phillip's dad used the services of the funeral home closer to her home than the one we had chosen for Phillip. While planning her services, the funeral planners offered recently delivered new prayer cards and guest registry books for his consideration. We would be the first family to use the new designs. When Pete saw the cards and book, he knew they were divinely inspired. There was "Stairway to Paradise," the Kinkade print, on the front of both. Phillip was welcoming his beloved grandmother to paradise.

∞

CHAPTER 8

Heaven or Kentucky

*"Friendship improves happiness, abates misery,
by doubling our joys and dividing our grief."*
—JOSEPH ADDISON

The day of the car accident, thankfully, my home was filled with family and friends who had become family. One of the people who contacted me by phone was a dear friend, Mary Jo McCabe. She is a well known spiritual teacher and gifted woman well connected beyond the five senses to the wisdom of greater awareness and spiritual guidance. Twenty years earlier, she had changed my life by introducing me to loving psychic experiences which led me to a greater love of God. I wondered about the great mysteries of life in my search for a God I could relate to. She was the first to open the door of learning that forever changed my view from a judgmental God to a loving God who is present in all things. Also, she was full of life and laughter and made living a more connected Christian life possible for me.

When Mary Jo phoned from Florida, she offered her condolences and asked if I wanted her to share what feeling and messages she was getting from Phillip. Of course I said yes, because I knew it was delivered with love. Phillip knew about my classes with her and would know to communicate with her to get a message to me.

She said that Phillip was with a younger girl named Jessica. A few years earlier, a group of teenagers were at a party and loading into cars to go to a second party as teenagers often do. The driver of one of the cars, Jessica, invited Phillip to ride with them but he chose to go in another car.

Minutes later, Jessica was killed in a car accident. Phillip always carried her picture on his key chain and one on his visor, referring to her as his 'Angel.' It is comforting to know that she was there to greet him.

Another thing Mary Jo shared was that Phillip was in Kentucky which I thought was a really strange thing to say. I remember my dear friend, Nina who also studied with Mary Jo saying, "Well, you go to Heaven or you go to Kentucky." In my deep despair, I actually chuckled thinking it was the most ridiculous thing I could imagine hearing.

When my eldest daughter, Jamie, arrived from Ohio, after driving for hours with her husband and two daughters, I remembered what Mary Jo had said. When I shared it with Jamie, her eyes lit up, and she told me that was true. When they were driving through Kentucky on the way to Louisiana, she sensed Phillips's presence and heard him say that he was alright. She said he was smiling, eyes twinkling as usual, giving her a sense that everything was great. What a surprise to find out that there was a real possibility that he was somehow in Kentucky. Even though I did not understand it, along with everyone in the room, I found it comforting.

It is possible that when we die, we will be surprised at what we did not see with our limited physical vision. After all, quantum physics is proving that we are all atoms vibrating together. Depending on how those atoms are arranged determines our depth of vision or inability to see with the human eye. Jamie could see with her sixth sense or what is sometimes called the "mind's eye." When the one who has made the transition talks to us, it's not as if we converse like on the earth, but more a telepathic connection which is no less real that if they were here. When I received this information from my daughter, I was thankful that I had shared my spiritual education with my children. She was unafraid to come into a room and tell that story. Her own inner knowledge empowered her to say what was true from her heart, as tearful as it was, and as strange as it may have seemed. She and Phillip shared a unique connection while he was here, why would it be a surprise that they shared it from another existence? Twice later, Phillip would use Jamie and Nina to get a message through to his grieving mother.

∞

CHAPTER 9

Disappointment on Both Sides

"Death is simply a shedding of the physical body like the butterfly shedding its cocoon. It is a transition to a higher state of consciousness where you continue to perceive, to understand, to laugh, and to be able to grow."
—DR. ELIZABETH KÜBLER-ROSS

Although I know that we are all eternally connected, the power of the physical presence is the most compelling force there is when suffering the loss of a loved one. I felt as if my heart had been ripped out of my chest for quite some time. Anxiety attacks, suicidal thoughts, and times of wailing and gnashing of teeth, (a phrase I'd learned in Sunday school) were standard operating procedure for me.

I have always been a strong woman with a determined spirit, who never considered medication for anything. Now I was debilitated. My daughter Stephanie's husband Benji, a nurse practitioner, led a drug intervention one Sunday afternoon at our Sunday dinner. While most interventions are to help one get off of drugs, this one was staged to get me on them. With their encouragement, I visited my primary care physician who wrote a prescription for one of the newer anti-depressants. I chose it because it had fewer side effects, and because it was not considered to be habit forming.

I suggest that if you have lost someone and feel you may never be yourself again, you should discuss this with your doctor or health care professional. Many well meaning friends offered their personal medication. I took a sleeping pill obtained from a friend before visiting the doctor which caused me to climb the walls instead of getting any sleep. Some medications have serious side effects like suicidal tendencies. I was already thinking suicide; I did not need anything to magnify that thought. My physician also prescribed a tranquilizer and advised me to get it filled whether I thought I needed it or not. She expressed concern that I had to endure Phillip's birthday, Mother's Day and holidays, without Phillip's physical presence. While I took the daily medication for a year, I took the tranquilizer only twice. A year's commitment on medication made sense to me and I made a decision to stop at that point.

Afterward I discovered that I still had to endure his birthday, Mother's Day, and holidays without medication. However, I knew that I was better equipped to do it after that first year. If you or someone you know needs medication, please do not judge the decision as being weak, or the medication as unnecessary. Refrain from playing doctor at such a vulnerable time.

In the beginning of this book, I asked you to suspend judgment. The request stands forever whether you are judging someone's methods to assuage grief, a rebellious teenager, or an irritating sibling. You cannot know another's pain. For a week, try to observe the "should" and "should not" statements you make about things others say or do. Then try to reserve comment when you catch yourself being judgmental. Notice how it feels to practice presence without judgment. To allow the space for individuality and alternate possibilities is especially helpful in times of suffering.

∞

I am not a religious person but I am a very spiritual person. I recommend that whether you consider yourself either, to find a place of support for your beliefs and dreams, a community that encourages you to your highest and best without judgment, no matter what you are going through.

After weeks of absence, I returned to Unity Church of Christianity, where I had attended for the past ten years. Each Sunday we end our service by reciting a beautiful prayer of protection. I was thankful to be part of such a loving community of friends who came to my side with food and help in ways I may never recall. Unity reminds us that the most important thing we can do on this earth is to love one another. Returning to church was like returning to a safe place that could help meet my needs at this desperate time. Seeing my church friends was helpful and supportive even though they did not know what to say. They did not have to say anything; it was evident in their eyes.

Joining hands and reciting the prayer of protection which ends with "Wherever we are, God is and all is well" has always brought me comfort in times of stress. This particular day, I couldn't stop wanting to be with Phillip. I did not care who was on this planet with me, I just wanted to be with him. I was saying the words to affirm that where Phil is and where I am, God is. All was not well. It was not enough. My tears would not stop.

When I returned home, I continued to wail, that nasty crying that seeps from deep within the soul. The next morning Jamie called and said that the night before in a dream, instead of showing himself smiling and joking as usual, Phillip appeared seemingly disappointed and sad. He told her that he couldn't stand to see me in the state I was in. Here was my daughter calling from Ohio, having no idea about my previous day, delivering a message that let me know I had been observed; someone is watching. Of course, the last thing I want to do is sadden or disappoint any of my children wherever they may be, so it gave me new found courage to get through a few more weeks.

Once again, I had one of those days when I felt that torment again and couldn't get a grip on myself or my emotions. Days later, Nina came for a short visit. She had a dream that tall lanky Phillip sat in her lap, put his arm around her and told her that he couldn't stand to see me in the state I was in. When I asked her when the dream occurred, again it was the day I was emotionally out of control. Someone is watching and expects better of me.

A third time, I had only recently met a woman who shared with me that she had a dream about my son and me. Not knowing how this would be received, I said, "I have two sons one on this side and one on the other." She surprised me when she said, "The one on the other side." Again she related to me how Phillip had told her that she had to let me know that I needed to stop grieving. Of course, at the time she had the dream, I once again had been "snot slinging nasty crying" as I grew to call it.

These encounters are no accident and are totally unscripted. They are a loving attempt by my son to let me know that he knows and cares about how I am doing. It has given me such strength at difficult times, knowing he has a higher expectation for me in the grieving process. While I honor that process, I hope to honor his wishes by moving forward with courage and strength no matter how much I cry. It's his attempt to allow me to get to know him in a different way.

∞

CHAPTER 10

Loving Help from Unexpected Sources

*"We understand why children are afraid of darkness...
but why are men afraid of light?"*

—PLATO

My mentor and spiritual counselor, Mary Jo McCabe came from her new home in Florida to visit the day after Phillip's funeral. She offered to come into town for the funeral services or afterward. I chose the day after so that she could sit with our family to share any messages from Phillip. You may or may not be open to this kind of communication, but we were comforted to have it available and to know that it was possible.

We sat in my living room while Vivienne took notes to hear any words that Phillip chose to share with us. There were many loving and insightful messages, one of which was that I would go on a trip in a few weeks. A friend whom Phil loved had invited me to go with him to Seattle and I had declined. I was the only one who knew about the invitation spoken to me privately. I guess someone was listening. Phillip encouraged me to go. Hesitantly, I contacted my friend, Tag, who kindly made the arrangements.

A month after the funeral, I was in Seattle where there were two incidents that Phil used to communicate to us. First, we were on a ferry to Victoria Island and I looked out the window into the water only to see a beautiful rainbow, seemingly only outside my window. Without giving clues, I asked Tag to look and tell me what he saw. He acknowledged the appearance of the rainbow, too. I had earlier asked Phillip to give me a sign that he was well and in my heart I knew this was my answer.

Later we were riding a bus up to Mt. Ranier when the guide announced that our stop would be in Paradise where we would be allowed to exit and spend time. When I got off the bus and walked a few yards, before me was a stairway surrounded by wildflowers, almost identical to Kinkade's painting. It took my breath away with its beauty. When we tried to take a picture, the batteries were dead in the camera although they worked when we went back down the mountain. I suppose it was for our eyes only. A photograph may not have done it justice.

Imagine my feeling of connection and love for Phillip as I stood in Paradise. Thank God I hadn't missed the opportunity to come to this place. It was tranquil and filled with butterflies and birds. Tag invited me at the lowest time in my life to receive this gift of love from a son to his mother.

Another interesting message from Phillip through Mary Jo was one concerning an attic. He insisted on speaking about an attic even though no one in the room understood the message. Nonetheless, Vivienne wrote it down. When the note was shared with her Dad, he was quite surprised. When he left for San Diego before Phillip's accident he customarily left a list of things for Phillip to do. Typically he would do none of the things or he might do one or two. This time he completed all the tasks except the one in the attic. The message was clearly for his father to let him know he didn't get that one done, and it still needed to be completed. For you skeptics out there, let me say that Phillip's father, Pete, is the most skeptical person you would ever meet. He's certainly skeptical about things without hard data. Losing his son has introduced him to things that under other circumstances he would not embrace, yet they are so obvious that he can't miss them.

∞

Weeks after that fateful night, Pete called to tell me another comforting experience. He taught the boys so much about birds and how much delight he got from watching and studying their habits. From the time they were born, Phillip and Tyler were mini ornithologists. Our backyard was a sanctuary usually filled with flight and chirping, delightfully observed by our family, especially the guys. Pete told me that a hawk had been following his path to work with his flight and would land in the back of the house, peeking into the window as if looking at the Stairway to Paradise Kinkade print. He noticed this hawk during his daily activities, driving around the small town and came to find it helpful in dealing with his grief. To this day, he says that when he's down and missing his son, he steps into the backyard, speaks to Phillip and a hawk shows up.

Our boys and their friends loved our yard for their games and boyhood activities. While they were growing up, when they were stressed about something, they would go into the yard, build a ramp or something of the sort and jump it with one of the many motorized vehicles we had for them to enjoy. Part of the fun was building the ramp in a better way to prevent destruction and create more risk, trying it again and again. Many times I have seen them play roughly in the yard after seemingly expending all their energy in a competitive game at school. Somehow they'd find more energy to work out the stress of the day. Physical exercise seemed a great way to deal.

After Phillip's transition, Pete observed seven young men, no longer boys, actively engaged in outdoor activities when he observed seven hawks sitting in a tree overlooking them. Normally hawks do not travel in flocks and are quick to leave when there's noise. These seven hawks, one for each young man, sat there overlooking them for hours. We may never know the significance of one hawk for each young man; nonetheless, Pete found great comfort in seeing those birds. When he described the picture to me, I could feel the love he was feeling from something bigger than the both of us. I too was grateful for the slight reprieve from our heartache.

∞

Tyler, my youngest son, was understandably lost during those first months. We allowed him to stay out of school for a semester to try and regain his balance. He spent time with mutual friends that he and Phillip shared and with family. He was always a "show me" kind of guy who needs proof. One weekend a group went to a hunting camp. When he got home he came to my house to tell me what happened as he returned. He was driving down the interstate at 65 MPH and said to Phillip, "You are always giving other people signs. I need a sign that you are okay." Within minutes, a car passed with a small boy sitting in the back seat, window rolled down, and head stuck out. The boy seemed to look directly at him, smiled, and flashed the peace sign. Tyler knew it was the sign he requested from his brother. After all, when do you see a car going down the interstate traveling over 65 MPH with a kid hanging out the back window flashing the same sign Phillip used when greeting you from a distance?

A week later he was with their friend Mark who told him that he thought that Tyler would hear from Phillip through someone flashing him the peace sign or something Phillip did. Imagine how surprised Mark was to find out it had already happened. It seemed to be a turning point for helping Tyler deal with his grief. I am thankful that he felt safe to share this to help others as well.

∞

Mary, who works at the hair salon I frequent, lost her son to leukemia. When I have an appointment and talk about my experiences she seems to find comfort that her son, Jamon, is in a special place. As a smoker, she goes outside often during the day. She told me that after my visits over the months following my son's crossing, a hawk would circle above their parking lot for a day or so. Her hawk sighting confirmed Pete's experience.

One day as I was leaving, she grabbed my hand and asked if maybe Jamon, had a message for her? I walked out the door and halfway to my car I heard a voice say, "Tell my mother to change the oil in her car now." I stopped in my tracks, sort of shook my head, and kept walking to my car; I was overcome with guilt knowing that while I thought the message ridiculous, any message from a loved one is comforting. Going back inside I felt silly when I told Mary. Her face lit up as she told me that on the way to work that morning she was concerned that her oil change was dangerously overdue. I am sure she took care of it immediately. This may seem trivial but Mary's smile and the peace in her face made me glad I risked looking silly as I closed the door to leave.

I urge you to pay attention to what nature or others may be saying to you to help you find a connection for healing. Had Pete not been astute, he would have missed the healing opportunity offered by the hawks. I know our loved ones don't stalk us and pay attention to our intimate moments. Just like when our loved ones were here, they are with us yet separate from us. Most of the daily petty things we do and worry about certainly are not important in the big picture of life. What's important is that we know we are loved from the other side and that they know we love them. It's never too late to make that known. You can have a heart to heart conversation that can lighten any burden you may have. Just try it, no matter how silly it feels, you might be pleasantly relieved.

∞

When Phillip's car accident occurred, Stephanie and Benji were expecting their second child. She had not yet announced it to the family. The week after the funeral, she invited me to attend the ultrasound appointment with her to see the baby. As the technician scanned her stomach, I noticed immediately there was no apparent heartbeat. My heart went out to Stephanie; here was another tragedy so soon after our trauma. We sobbed together as this added to our loss. A month or so later, the same ultrasound experience was once again repeated and they lost another pregnancy. You can only imagine their disappointment and heartbreak after this news.

While they were so thankful for Treg, their son, they really wanted another child. She said that her love for Treg was so amazing and strong that she wanted to share it with another child as well. Two months after these two miscarriages, Linda Hullinger, a well known medium (someone who can facilitate messages from the other side) came to my home to meet with a few mothers and singled me out to say that Phillip had a message for Stephanie. I listened attentively and in awe as she said that he told her that recently the same soul had tried to come to us twice.

The soul was in such a hurry to get here that "he" was trying to come before "he" was ready and that Phillip kept pulling him back and nurturing him. He said that I should tell Stephanie that the third time is the charm and that "he" would be fine. I was so shocked by this information. Considering how traumatic the losses were to Stephanie, I found it difficult to tell her. What if I was wrong? Hurting Stephanie, by giving her false hope, would be even more painful.

At one of our Sunday lunches, I couldn't contain the information about the anxious soul who wanted to come to her any longer. Instead of being stressed by the news, she calmly told me how thankful she was to hear it and that it would give her the courage to have another child. The relief was apparent on her face, even though when she became pregnant a few months later, she would have numerous ultrasounds and need countless reassurance that things were truly fine.

Drew Phillip Arboneaux made his entrance on this planet, November 1, All Saints Day. He is everything Phillip said and much more. I am so grateful for the reassurance before the conception, and the fulfillment of Phillip's promise, when I hold this beautifully perfect child of God in my arms. How can we ever think there is no Higher Power? It's only through love and miracles these things exist. Although my logical mind could continue to question, my soul knows it would not be helpful to do so.

∞

In 1983 the book *Many Lives Many Masters* was released, changing my life forever. Dr. Brian Weiss, a renowned psychiatrist with a skeptical and scientific mind, wrote about his own transformative experience in treating a patient who was not making progress using traditional treatment. He decided to use hypnotherapy only to discover there was much more to this person's life than either of them ever imagined or expected. As a traditional psychotherapist, Dr. Weiss was astonished and skeptical when one of his patients began recalling past-life traumas that seemed to hold the key to her recurring nightmares and anxiety attacks. His skepticism was eroded, however, when she began to channel messages from "the space between lives," which contained remarkable revelations about Dr. Weiss's family and his dead son.

Many Lives Many Masters confirmed my suspicions that life is larger than we can imagine with connections that transcend time and space. In 2008 the book celebrated twenty five years in publication and Dr. Weiss appeared on Oprah. Although I personally met Dr. Weiss at a workshop years earlier, seeing him that day on Oprah held new meaning since Phillip's transition.

I find great comfort in knowing that we may have lived before and may choose to return to earth if that is what our soul needs in order to refine our journey to our Source. I highly recommend you read this fascinating recount of a most amazing experience. It might change your life forever and more importantly, if you've lost a loved one, help your grief journey. For me, it was a hundred "Grace Moments" rolled into one.

To learn more about where our memories are stored and what our connection to our past may be, I continue my studies as a licensed hypnotherapist. I am grateful for being exposed to such alternative thinking compared to the religious and philosophical tenets taught to me by my church, my community, and my parents. Having someone so near and dear make a transition that was unconscionable to me, forces me to really be present in each moment, to notice my own small voice within that guides me when I am quiet enough to listen, and to be more compassionate to the way people choose to handle their lives. Like me, you have a daily choice to live in loss or live in love. We each must discern for ourselves what seems true to our inner knowing. I encourage you to expand your awareness of what life might be in order to fully appreciate the magnificence of what it means to be alive forever. We can be truly alive as long as we create, participate, and try to lovingly appreciate all that life has to teach us.

The way we choose to create our lives through our thoughts and actions can make the difference in the richness of our lives. The one thing we can control is quality of life. It helps me to see quantity of life as eternal. Choose with the intent to, among other things, embrace a higher consciousness, know love, connect with others, and make a positive impact; you may actually pass this way again.

My sister spent the night at my home when an unexpected yet undeniable experience occurred that was so profound we could hardly speak about it. Sleeping in the downstairs bedroom while I slept upstairs gave her easy access to the kitchen and morning coffee which I expected to smell when I awakened. Instead of breakfast aromas, there were no smells or sounds; this caused me to jump from my bed and run to check on her. On the way into the room passing a table, I noticed my glasses on the floor, picked them up and returned them to the table, thinking the cat had knocked them off. When I entered the room, I saw Charlene propped up on pillows, the covers to her chin and her big brown eyes wide with wonder. She said to me, "I will never doubt any of the stories about Phillip's presence again." She shared with me that during the night she was awakened by the touch of a hand on her shin. She immediately knew it was Phillip. She told him to stop, she was trying to sleep. What happened next frightened her beyond imagination. Instantly placed on her feet, she found herself standing beside the bed as he urged her forward through my home. Although feeling like he was trying to move her upstairs toward me, she stopped at the foot of the staircase. She turned to him saying, "Phillip, are you worried about your mother? She is going to be fine. I will make sure that she is going to be fine." With that he was gone while she walked back into the bedroom and stayed awake the rest of the night. She was so shaken that I had her write it down so nothing would be forgotten. She asked me not to mention it since she was sure people would think she was crazy.

I am reminded of Dr. Weiss' repetitive recitation of his professional credentials and highly regarded reputation in each of his books to remind readers once again of his sanity and professional dedication to the truth. Dr. Weiss' version of "I'm not crazy." My sister and I never spoke about it until this writing when I asked her permission to tell it in her words because it could help so many. A former Mayor of one of the fastest growing cities in our state, as well as the principle in her own insurance agency, with the Grace of God she was able to allow herself to be vulnerable. More importantly, she is a loving mother who hopes to help other families in their grief. I did vow to attest along with many that she is one of the smartest, wittiest, and loving women I know. Notice I did not say crazy.

When she left that morning, I discovered a broken arm on the glasses I had placed back on the table. Obviously she had knocked them off and stepped on them on her way to the staircase. I will keep those glasses forever as a reminder of Phillip's attempt to take care of me. We are not alone and not crazy, but lovingly connected.

∞

CHAPTER 11

Wesley's Presence

"Do not stand at my grave and weep; I am not there. I do not sleep. I am a thousand winds that blow. I am the diamond glints on snow. I am the sunlight on ripened grain. I am the gentle autumn's rain. When you awaken in the morning's hush, I am the swift uplifting rush of quiet birds in circled flight. I am the soft stars that shine at night. Do not stand at my grave and cry; I am not there. I did not die."
—ANONYMOUS

Trudi's family lived across the street when our children were younger. Her son, Wesley, had crossed over a short time prior. Like Phillip, he was also close to his mother and she was still managing the suffering. She introduced me to Betty whose son, Cade, had crossed over in a car accident.

After going to the movies with his family, they had returned home, and Cade left for a short ride from which he never returned. Betty had dark circles under her eyes and was so thin that she looked as if you could blow on her and she would topple over. She seemed hardly able to function because she was so burdened with grief. Seeing these two frightened me, yet strengthened my resolve to help them while trying desperately to help myself. When they were leaving, I was so shaken by Betty's pain that I desperately wanted to help all of us. We had joined a club that no one wanted to be a part of. Our "Birds" had flown and we were left behind to feather our nests. During the following year these friends proved to be instrumental in my journey toward healing. I often think that Wesley led his mother to introduce us to support one another.

Long before Phillip's transition, Wesley told me he was helping children make their transition to the other side. Again, it's not like lips moving and the type of talking we are accustomed to. It is sort of telepathic communication. Trying to explain this is like asking me to conjugate a sentence in Aramaic or a language I do not comprehend. I shared that information from Wesley with his mother who thought it so appropriate since he always loved children on this side as well. On the day of Phillip's transition, Wesley's mother was sitting at her computer when a pop-up appeared saying, "I am helping them adjust to a l..." The word was incomplete. She sat wondering what it meant when her phone rang to tell her of Phillip's accident. She and her husband Rodney came to my home where I held onto them and wept, knowing they really knew how I felt. Wesley was helping Phillip as his parents were helping me.

Wesley was much like Phillip: popular, fun, funny, and reckless, with that dynamite personality you couldn't resist. The last time I saw Wesley before he crossed over, he showed me a picture of his little son who looked as if he had spit him out, so much like him. His eyes twinkled as he showed the picture and laughed that he also had a redhead son just like my Tyler. I remembered when he used to play in my yard as a small child. He was the oldest boy and quite the leader. Wesley played in a band, loved music (especially Lynyrd Skynyrd's song "Free Bird"). When I was writing this book, he came to stand beside my bed and said that the name would be "The Free Bird Flies." When he appeared, he looked as if I could see through him, like others who have appeared to me from the other side.

Although this infrequently happens now, it no longer frightens me to have them show up. Maybe you think I was dreaming. It doesn't matter because the love I feel is overwhelming, not like anything I have felt before...it's indescribable. There was no doubt it was Wesley.

Another day I was really tired and said to Phillip and Wesley that I needed to know they were with me. When I turned on the television immediately following my request, it was on a station I do not watch and a woman had just begun singing "His Eye is On the Sparrow." I believe this book you hold in your hand is a joint effort by me and loving unseen helpers who can aid us in looking at death differently than we have before. It is as much of a mystery as ever. It would be more helpful to be more enlightened about death so that we all might lovingly grow and learn. Certainly we all must deal with it. Discussion may possibly serve to lessen the pain. More than likely it will help facilitate our lessons in love. Whenever Wesley wants our attention, the song "Free Bird" plays on the radio at home or in the car. Sometimes even in the most unusual circumstances.

In March of 2007 my friend, Joe Liss and I attended a Beatles Rewind Play in New Orleans. Joe is a CPA who likes lots of information, a procedure, and a plan. In other words, he is another skeptic like Pete.

I was daydreaming during the concert and wondered whether or not I should continue conducting the monthly grief workshops Linda Hullinger and I had started four months prior. You know how you might have these doubtful thoughts and feelings about something you are doing and you ask, 'What's the point?" Suddenly, in the middle of a Beatles song, the band began to play; you guessed it, "Free Bird." They played a few bars, stopped and said, "What are we doing? That's by Lynyrd Skynyrd." Immediately they once again began to play a Beatles song. Joe looked at me inquisitively. I could only smile. When the concert was over, hearing the explanation, Joe became another unsuspecting skeptic with a paranormal experience he couldn't deny. Wesley's way of saying, "Happy Birthday, Mr. Joe and yes, Ms. Bert, continue the workshops."

When you begin to accept the help from God provided by the other side, it can serve to make the things happening in your life make more sense. Wesley's Dad, Rodney, is a real estate developer. Most of his projects go smoothly and profitably. He recently purchased some property to develop a subdivision named Wesley Place and found obstacles being thrown in his path at many junctures. Those obstacles came at a time when he was really missing Wesley's physical presence and he was beginning to fall into depressing thoughts. Suddenly he realized that those obstacles served as an impetus to keep him involved, challenged, and it motivated him to keep everyone involved in the project moving forward. He was thankful to Wesley for not allowing him to sit down and be a victim but to take a proactive approach to finishing a commitment that otherwise would have been stalled. Reframing those challenges, seeing them as a blessing from Wesley rather than a curse from the Universe, reminded Rodney of the stamina and determination needed to live his life. Sensing that Wesley was behind the motivation made work more meaningful and productive. We often hear how, when we change our thinking, we can change our lives. This is the practice in action and I am thankful that this masculine, formerly skeptical, man is unafraid to share information to help you understand that, even in the most difficult circumstances, life can continue in a loving way.

∞

CHAPTER 12

Life's Spiritual Lessons

"Death ... is no more than passing from one room into another. But there's a difference for me, you know. In that other room I shall be able to see."
—HELEN KELLER

Twelve years before Phillip's accident, fifteen women in our area, took a spiritual development class with Mary Jo at The McCabe Institute. The goal of this class, which met weekly for two and a half years, was to help us get in touch with the Divine gifts we all share. A new experience for each, it was designed to help us use more than our five senses to make decisions and take action in our daily lives.

Spending one night a week studying and sharing life experiences at The McCabe Institute, we learned that we are all connected to God no matter where we are on our continuing path to completion. We also learned that we have gifts we can choose to access to help us on this life path. It opened a door for me to the ones who have crossed over.

Judy Collier, after losing her only son, Kyle, in a car accident, attended those classes. Many times Kyle would speak to her through Mary Jo telling her stories and recounting things that were happening in her life that only Judy and her family could have known. Judy often would seem to be sitting in her chair listening, yet when Mary Jo was finished, would ask again if Kyle had a message for her. It was as if Kyle had said nothing. I now know the depth and width of a sorrow so painful it can render a mother unable to hear.

I saw Judy go from a stuttering ball of grief to an eloquent speaker, helping mothers like me on their grief journey. Her book, *Quit Kissing My Ashes*, recounts a story that actually happened to me and one I shared with the class and now with you.

Awakened from a sound sleep, a woman who had crossed over in a terrible car accident with two of her five children, was standing next to my bed. I hardly knew her when she was on this side. I saw her transparent outline standing next to my bed when she called my name and told me hers. Her request that I deliver a message to her husband was one of those moments that impacted my life forever. I can never again honestly deny this kind of communication is possible. Questioning how he would know it was really a message from her, she held out her hand to show me a shiny pin that she was sure would identify her. Although the experience was paranormal, I felt peaceful in her presence.

I did not contact her husband for three days since I was hesitant to speak about it and terrified of his response. After not sleeping for two nights, I prayed for restful sleep promising to deliver the message the next day. With much trepidation, I wrote everything down, met with her husband, and acknowledged that he might consider it a little crazy.

He had gone into their children's rooms, sat on their beds and thought, "People are always telling me they are ok. How can I know that?" When I told him about the shiny pin in her hand, reassurance was evident in his face. He placed cubic zirconium angel pins on each of his family as a remembrance. She answered the questions he had posed the very day of her appearance to me.

I assumed that he might not believe me because of his strong Catholic beliefs. Feeling the overwhelming love and power of that message brought tears to both of us. Truth delivered in an undeniably loving way can sometimes set us free from limiting beliefs that do not serve to help us heal. I could have eased his grief three days earlier had I gone to him right away.

It's not a surprise I was sleep deprived for days when, out of sheer exhaustion, I finally submitted to the request. Looking foolish is not something we like to risk.

While in this class, some of us lost parents, one lost her only son months earlier, while others changed jobs. All were challenged by life. Sharing with one another this spiritual level of communication, and a new way of looking at life, helped us grow emotionally and spiritually. I am so grateful for these friendships where we supported and encouraged each other to be open to all the love from both sides of the veil beyond our physical existence.

Since Phillip's crossing, I may have an opportunity to help others in their grief. In my human existence I have ignored this possibility for so long and now there's someone on the other side that I have to get to know in a different way for my own healing. A new sense of compassion has awakened within my spirit. I pray daily to have the wisdom, strength, and courage to do whatever I am called to do.

∞

When our spiritual classes ended at the McCabe Institute, a small group began meeting in my home. At these gatherings, a member of the group, Linda Hullinger, would allow us to ask questions of our Guides and loved ones. More comfortable with our roles as teachers and students, we welcome any information to help us on our life's journey toward lovingly being the best we can be. Linda's gift was to answer these questions with such clarity of direction that only our loved ones or Guides would have known, letting us know our time together had value and we have help from unseen sources.

Ten years after the formation of the original class, four remaining members regularly met to celebrate our individual birthdays. It's hard to give up sharing our lives as "soul sisters." In January of 2006, we gathered at my home for Nina's birthday celebration. After dinner we sat around on my sofas while Linda shared the messages she received.

In the earlier years we had little success recording our meetings even though the equipment seemed to be working properly. Assuming the messages were only meant for the people in the room at that moment, we gave up trying to record. For the first time in years we resurrected the tape recorder and it actually recorded the messages. Nina took the tape home, transcribed it, and sent each of us a copy. I did not read mine, placed it into a drawer, and forgot about it.

I have been told by teachers on both sides that our soul sometimes knows when we are called to continue our lives in another way. Sometimes it is consciously expressed, other times not. Retrospectively, Phil's comment on the Kinkade print was a premonition. In the second year after his transition, I was cleaning and found the following transcription from the meeting six months before his accident.

Let's talk about Phillip. Poor boy is suffering with this weather. I feel pressure, watering and stinging eyes. He is getting ready to examine this thing with his brother. He would never hurt Tyler but it would be good if you could guide them to do their own thing. Phillip is moving forward and upward and Tyler is happy where he is. Phillip doesn't want to leave him behind but he says he has to go forward; there are things waiting for him. He has a higher purpose. He doesn't know what it is but he is being called and he knows he has to do something. He can't hang around waiting for Tyler to catch up with him.

I thought Phillip wanted to move into a new apartment, not off the planet! I do not believe this was given to alarm me. I found it at the right time to bring comfort in knowing he knew he had a higher calling and how much he loved his brother. Other mothers have told me of conversations they've had with their children which later proved prophetic in letting them know that on some level they may have known it was their time to go.

Trudi, Wesley's mother, asked if Linda Hullinger would meet with us to help with healing. I explained that she no longer did medium work, choosing instead to concentrate on her writing. Out of respect for her decision, I did not ask Linda for help. A few weeks after Phil's transition, my small spiritual group gathered at my home. It should not have been a surprise when Linda, trusting her guidance, volunteered to meet as often as I chose with whomever I chose.

∞

CHAPTER 13

The Group No One Wants to Join

*"Life isn't about waiting for the storm to be over,
it's about learning how to dance in the rain."*

—VIVIAN GREEN

Getting to know our loved ones in a different way is not nearly as fulfilling as touching them and sharing a physical presence. It is a way to maintain our soul connection even though the body is not here. Gathering with others who had experienced loss was essential. Sharing our physical suffering, coupled with the insightful communication from our loved ones, somehow made things more bearable. At first is seems there can never be enough connection. As the connection is affirmed by hearing heartfelt messages and seeing signs of their presence, the process becomes a more peaceful part of life. You realize there is more going on than just trying to keep in touch. Life must continue on both sides.

Some find it helpful to go to the cemetery if there has been a burial and talk with their loved one. Personally, I do not find that comforting. What I do find comforting is the knowledge that he is occasionally watching and sharing my experiences. I do not have to understand it with my human mind, only to know it in my eternal soul.

Although I knew Trudi would be in the group no one wants to join, I trusted that the others would appear as needed. After all, the intent was to help anyone who needed help with heartache. Over the next few months, mothers who had lost children would hear from their children, either in the workshops Linda and I led, or in small gatherings in my home. Some parents got what they needed and never returned. Some were not spiritually, psychologically, or emotionally ready for such an encounter. Each one returned at a later time. Whatever the experience for the individual mother, there was always a common bond of love and tenderness shared by everyone present. We were all reaching out to find comfort in the presence of one another. Individually, we suffered; together we found an unexpected, if only slight, measure of relief.

Sometimes the pain can be so heavy that only a tiny bit of help is felt; it is especially significant when you have reached a point where you can accept the help. When you begin to experience those "Grace Moments" of loving knowingness, of a new awareness, of transcending this human experience you might feel a direct line to the God of your understanding. Divine Love meets human thought and something more peaceful is experienced. I am eternally grateful for Grace Moments even if I do not understand them fully.

Skepticism is welcome concerning our process. For some of the workshop attendees these communications would have been declared impossible had we not experienced unmanageable grief.

When you read these stories, you may be reminded of something you long ago stored in your memory. When it happened, you thought it too weird to discuss, may have been afraid of social retribution, or may have just denied it totally. You may not have any of those memories but will discover as you grow in your spiritual journey that there is life after loss. May you find the strength, courage, and permission to experience and share with others your deepest fears, while recognizing your personal "Grace Moments."

∞

In October of 2006, my friend's daughter brought me a rescue kitten that won my heart. Due to his abrupt entrance into the world, and my experience with abrupt exits, we made an appropriate pair. Not sure if I had the capacity for caring, I was apprehensive about what would happen next for the kitten since he looked somewhat frightened and in great need of tender care. I named him Putch, Phillip's nickname given to him by his friend Mark who somehow has a gift for making up names that seemed to stick.

Putch the cat and I struck up a relationship that nurtured us both. I wasn't sure how he would handle having strangers sharing his space on meeting night since he had only recently gotten used to me. I tried to close him outside our meeting room when the mothers arrived for their first meeting. He screamed so loudly that we could not hear our own conversation. I asked my guests' permission and allowed him inside.

Linda would address each mother for a while, then another mother's child would get her attention and she would wrap up the current message, and move to the other mother. There was no pattern to the movement around the room. The message might change from one side of the room to the other. After coming inside, Putch moved to the center of the group, looked around and quietly jumped into the lap of the mother whose child was sending a message at that moment. Although the messages were in random order, he would move into the lap of the mother whose child was speaking as Linda began to address her. He did this all night changing laps when another child would communicate. The only mother whose lap he did not sit in was the mother whose son did not like cats. Seemingly, he knew what was going on and lovingly wanted to participate.

Many times when only he and I are present, he will paw into the air as if he can see something I cannot see. Who knows what vibration animals are resonating with that allows them to see things our human eyes cannot? Observing Putch the cat has made me ponder that question on many occasions.

A mother whose son, Dane, crossed over two days after Phillip, joined our weekly group. Sherri would come into my home with the tense body posture each of us had at one time or another and sit quietly with her head down. When we began, Linda said that Dane was showing her a box of Special K cereal. She questioned whether or not Sherri was eating well.

Her interpretation was that Dane was trying to tell her to improve her nutritional intake. Sherri continued writing until her head shot up, eyes sparkling when Linda suddenly said that Dane spun the box around and outlined the Big K. With a big smile and more relaxed posture, Sherri shared this story with us.

> Over the course of several years, Dane and I had dinner together once a week. On some of these occasions, I would be dropped off at the door of a store to retrieve an item needed at home. Dane would always wait for me in the car, in the driver's seat, watching for my exit; we would leave and continue on to the restaurant of our choice. One day recently, I quickly entered K-Mart for drinks needed at home. My heart was extremely heavy due to missing my son terribly. My mission was to get what I needed and leave very quickly before the uncontrollable tears started. Upon exiting I thought I saw Dane sitting in my car, watching for my exit, like many times before. As I quickly moved closer he faded. I told him that if he was really there that day that when we met with Linda he should say something about the Big K.

I can't explain the look of loving gratitude and tears of joy in his mother's eyes when she knew Dane was really with her. No one in that room knew the words Sherri was looking for, but Dane and God knew. Thankfully, Linda Hullinger used her gift to accurately affirm acknowledgment of Sherri's request to Dane. Everyone present sat there with awesome gratitude to know our sons were able to let us know so precisely that they were fine.

Meeting with Linda helped Sherri connect with an intuitive gift she has struggled to acknowledge. As a young child she knew things others didn't, yet like many, was frightened or discouraged by others to explore her gift until Dane's transition.

This past Christmas, we were once again trying to spend the holiday without emotional turmoil when Sherri's gift was once again awakened to service. The Christmas 2008 holiday season was beginning to be difficult for me. Sherri called to tell about a meditation she had where she saw a huge Christmas tree with live birds and beautiful decorations. Our boys and others were surrounding the tree with happy faces and seemingly joyful spirits.

She went to her computer and began to type, although, she knew the words were not hers, she wrote what she understood and sent it to me exclaiming her hesitation in sending out something so unpolished. I found comfort in knowing that someone was trying really hard to help us understand that if we choose, personal holidays can be experienced wherever we are. I share Sherri's gift with you for holiday peace.

"A Place Called Heaven"

*An enormous tree miles and miles tall encrusted with real stars
circling the majestic tree; Illuminating the Heavenly skies for all to see.
The stars twinkled in harmony ever so slightly;
providing a wealth of brilliance that shone very brightly.*

*Growing on this Heavenly tree were vast amounts of luscious fruit
creating a mouth watering treat;
shiny red apples, huge oranges and apricots, large clusters of grapes
cascading for several feet.
The fruit provided the most beautiful shades of color so vivid and bright;
luminous glistening in the starlight.
Beautiful species of live birds chosen for the pure pleasure of decorating this
majestic tree; placed at the most precise locations were perched perfectly.*

*Balance and scale they provided to the Heavenly tree;
proud to be chosen for all to see.
The branches were slightly bowed due to the beautiful ice crystals weight;
these magnificent ice crystals were all formed from tears of fate.*

Resembling beautiful prisms providing a divine rainbow of color;
the ice crystals magnify the splendor designed by the Great Sculptor.
Our beloved sons, as well as others, encircled this Heavenly tree;
messages radiate from each beckoning peace and tranquility.

It is equally apparent their love for everyone and all things;
this is the true Divine place of wondrous blessings.
This is the place called Heaven they want all to know;
this is the sacred legacy for all to bestow.

I thank God that Sherri was open to hearing from Divine guidance. Her action to write it exactly as it was delivered, acknowledgment of its potential comfort to others, and willingness to share it despite its imperfections gave me and others much needed strength.

∞

Betty's son acknowledged to Linda that he was present in the back seat of his mother's car, proudly supporting her decision to rescue a distraught woman earlier that day. Betty was in her office when a homeless woman abruptly entered the business, said she had been raped and asked Betty for help. Betty was shaken and confused at how the woman found her hard to reach office. She immediately moved to help her by driving her to a shelter. She had quickly returned to work and hastily come straight to our meeting, speaking to no one about it. Imagine the shock on her face when Cade communicated this message to Linda. Betty was so comforted to know that although she couldn't see him, he was present that day, telling her specifics about the helpful intervention that only she knew.

When people judge this beyond the physical communication from loved ones to be "of the devil," they have not seen how loving and Christlike this support can be. Providing genuine comfort, love, and hope to those in pain, it renews faith in the moment.

∞

Another unwilling club member was a former colleague who lost her daughter a few weeks before Phillip's transition. I remember the laughter and joy we shared working together at an annual trade show in New Orleans. Her adorable daughter was so personable and poised. Due to complications following an elective surgical procedure she made her transition.

During our conversation about the challenges we now face, I received helpful tips to help me continue to manage my grief. My former colleague stated that she does not allow herself to cry while sitting or lying down. Making that agreement with herself to only cry while standing up gave her the power to find the strength she needed in that moment. Now that might not seem like rocket science to most of you or an earth shattering statement, however, to me it was profound. I began to set that same boundary for myself and immediately felt empowered.

Prior to having this conversation, I wondered about parents of different religions who have lost a child. In our grief, could we find a common ground for healing regardless of our chosen name for God? As a Jehovah's Witness, my friend has beliefs much different than mine. The comfort we find in the God of each of our understanding, allowed us to respectfully share our heartfelt pain and grief management suggestions. When judgment is suspended, we become one.

I believe we are expected by our loved ones on the other side to learn to dance in the rain. Of course, grief has its demands, yet if we can somehow stay focused upon the love and joy offered to us, our ability to dance in the rain just may be possible.

∞

When one mother heard about our group she brought a picture that was taken at the scene of her son, Jeffrey's, accident. She and her husband gave me permission to share the picture of their son's spirit clearly showing his shoes and jeans. It provides evidence that we do not suffer but transcend when our departure comes.

The picture was taken by an off duty policemen with a disposable camera and developed at a local pharmacy. I interviewed him and was impressed with his calm demeanor, dedication to law enforcement, and kindness to a grieving mother. After a personal meeting, I wrote to get approval for how I understood the story. The policeman replied:

It was really nice to meet you and I am very sorry for the loss of your son. On the night of the accident May 1, 2002 I had just gotten off work and was getting ready to leave the police station when I heard the accident call come over another officer's radio. I heard the license plate called in off the car and was friends with the registered owner of the car. I believed that person may be involved in the accident and I responded to the scene to check. Once I arrived on scene, I noticed that the car contained 5 other friends that I knew and the registered owner wasn't involved. I did see that Jeffrey had died at the scene of the accident and three other passengers were seriously injured.

I began to take photographs of the accident scene. One of the photos was of Jeffrey after he was placed in a body bag. I got the photos developed a short time after the accident and several friends of the people involved wanted to see the pictures. I am not sure who actually noticed the picture of Jeffrey's spirit but it was brought to my attention. I looked at the pictures numerous times and didn't notice it until it was brought to my attention. I knew then that he was okay and in a better place. A short time later, his mother called about the picture. I had a copy made for myself, gave her the photo and negative so she could do what she wanted with it.

My other friend stayed on life support for 6 days and passed away on May 7, 2002. His parents donated his organs. This call was very difficult for me since I knew all the victims of the accident and was honored when asked to serve as a pallbearer for both guys. I had a difficult time dealing with this tragedy for a while and as months passed, my friend's parents received a letter from the LOPA (Organ Agency) and it detailed how his organs were used to give others a second chance at life. Two of the people that got those organs were police officers from Louisiana. I knew that when I read this letter that it was his way of letting me know that he was all right and also in a better place. I found a lot of comfort and closure in the picture of one friend and the letter about organs donation of the other.

You may doubt the validity of the picture; however, there is nothing you can say that will negate its authenticity to Jeffrey's parents and the policeman who took it. It's a gift that provides numerous "Grace Moments" for many who have lost loved ones. Maybe we will see more pictures like this in the future to provide more evidence about the circle of life.

Workshops brought others who were relieved to find a comfortable supportive environment to share their stories of connections with their loved ones. I love this refreshing story about flowers.

Here is Irene's story:

At our office we were interviewing people for a receptionist position. One new applicant brought a dozen pink roses and one yellow rose into the office. We made a few remarks like, "Bringing roses is a good way to land a job" but at the same time, we felt this action was really weird. Janet, our new applicant, placed these roses on the front desk as I went to greet her. She explained she had a rose garden, had picked the roses that very morning and thought we might enjoy them as she hated to see the roses lose their petals and go to waste. I placed the roses on my desk and there was an unbelievable scent that filled my room all day long. That afternoon a strange "sensation" came over me. I remembered a show that I love to watch, "Crossing Over" by John Edward. Many times he would say that the people he was getting messages from, who had crossed over, were showing him pink roses. This was a sign to send a message to their family of how very much they loved them. As soon as I remembered this, I absolutely, positively felt as though this was coming from Christie, my lost daughter, herself, with a special message to her mom to say she missed me and loved me. At this time, Michelle, my oldest daughter called and I immediately began telling her about the pink roses and my feeling it had something to do with Christie. She answered, "Well, good thing they aren't yellow roses, yellow roses are Christie's favorite."

I gasped and really held back tears. I had completely forgotten. I ran down to my assistant Tara's office and said we had to hire this new applicant. Tara has been with me through all my experiencing "crazy" signs from Christie, so she knew not to even think I was losing my mind. We hired Janet that day and she started on Friday, my day off. Tara called me saying that she told Janet the story of Christie's death and hoped I did not mind. She also went on to tell Janet the story about the roses and what I had felt. Janet told her she normally does not pick the roses in early morning, but something compelled her to do so that day of the interview. She also felt like she was receiving a message to bring these to someone she did not know. After dropping her daughter off at school that morning, she considered giving them to someone there, but something told her to bring them with her to the interview, even though she knew this would really look strange. Janet also told Tara that morning as I greeted her, she almost said, "The Lord told me to bring these to you." To my amazement, that one yellow rose in the very center of all the pink roses was the ONLY yellow rose that had bloomed in her garden that day.

No one could ever convince Irene that this was not a message from her daughter. More importantly, who with a loving heart would try to convince her differently? Irene had been asking for another sign because she had been missing Christie so much. Grateful for this sweet and heaven sent message, this mother's heart could feel the kind of love that heals.

∞

Photo of 2002 accident scene taken by Officer Duane Carpenter. On the ground is Jeffrey Louviere's covered body next to the two men on the left. Notice the ethereal form wearing Jeffrey's shoes and jeans to the right of the picture in front of the over-turned vehicle. The reverent way in which Officer Carpenter respectfully delivered this to the parents of Jeffrey Louviere in their time of grief reminds me to be grateful for the compassion bravely shown by members of the law enforcement community.

Left to Right: Phillip Fife, Jamie Rosado, Vivienne Fife, Stephanie Arboneaux, and Tyler Fife. Photo taken at the wedding of Pete and Sharon Fife, three months before Phillip's accident on July 23, 2006.

CHAPTER 14

In Memory of Phillip

"Live your life from love, not loss."
—PHILLIP DALE FIFE

A few years prior to Phillip's transition, my children gave me a Mother's Memory jar filled with notes of things they remembered about their childhood. It was the best Mother's Day present I ever received. I am grateful for unexpectedly finding that gift recently. As I sat in the center of my bed and dumped out the contents, I read each small folded note and carefully placed it back inside the jar. Some of them showed a side of me I might not be proud of. I saw the humor in the recollection from a child's point of view. All the memories were expressed with great love and affection. Despite my tears, there was joy in my heart. Having those memories from all the children, especially the ones from Phillip, was priceless.

I could have made my transition that night believing that my life was complete. Of course, I did not die that night or the next. However, getting up the next morning was easier. Those memories in my jar were now held in my heart. I had swiftly read those memories years before, placed them back in the jar and stored them away. Only after Phillip was gone did they hold special meaning for me. I vowed I would try to be more present with my children, friends, and family when making memories.

If you have not created a memory jar with your loved ones, friends, or significant others in your life, be encouraged to do it now. Share those memories with the intention to appreciate their views and to deepen your relationships.

∞

The first July 23 after Phil's transition was approaching. I could not imagine how I would spend that day. After much prayer, reflection, and many tears cried while standing, I took charge and sent out this email to my list of business associates, friends, and family.

My Dear Friends,

I am asking you to help me get through the anniversary day of my son Phillip's transition by performing a random act of kindness for someone on that day in his memory. I appreciate your willingness to do this and celebrate the service you will provide in loving kindness for someone on the planet while making someone in the Divine realm smile as well. I also ask you to pray for all the parents I have met in the last year who have lost children. They are inspirational, courageous, and have my utmost respect as we know the truth of the continuation of life through the most challenging experience we've had thus far.

May you and yours be safe and remember how precious life is.

With Gratitude,

Remembering Phillip's generosity and compassion for others inspired my request. One business associate and his family were out for ice cream. He walked up to a table surrounded by a family and invited them to order ice cream as his treat to commemorate Phillip. He wrote to me thanking me for the opportunity to do something that felt so rewarding. What a great model for his children to observe.

I received over fifty notes from the recipients of my first email followed by reports from others around the globe who received a forward. A woman in Europe did not share her random act, however wrote to express gratitude for the opportunity to participate. Each of them expressed condolences but more than that, they felt it was a great way to honor my son's life.

Vivienne lives and works in New York City. That summer she hosted Tyler as he attended NYU. Being together in the typically minimal Manhattan apartment made it hard not to discuss my email. Knowing their shared resolve to embrace the messages from Phillip was a random act of kindness to me.

Vivienne's reply:

Tyler and I decided that instead of marking the 23rd as the date of last year's loss, we are going to mark it as a year that we have had the strength and courage to go on and how we have all continually loved and supported each other. Also, it's been a year that Phil has repeatedly shown us that he is at peace in a better place.

Viv

∞

That first Christmas, the thought of getting together for our annual game night on Christmas Eve was excruciating. Our family is so competitive and it is only natural that we play games when we get together. One game includes using old fashioned wooden cups with a string and ball attached to see how many balls we can get into the cup. The rule was that the cups only came out on Christmas, no practicing during the year. We would laugh ourselves silly as annually we all went after Phil's record. I did not gather with my family that year.

The second Christmas after our loss, I was better able to take part in family gatherings. While I was still not ready to celebrate on our traditional Christmas Eve, I gathered the family together a few days before. It was my way of "easing" into it.

We lit a candle in memory of Phillip and talked about some of our funnier moments together. I enjoyed it because it showed me that they were acting on the decision to celebrate Phillip's life. Choosing to focus on the fun, great memories, and laughter they shared rather than his loss, created a safe space to cry. I am grateful for their openness and direct approach when talking about their brother.

Every family and each family member must deal with grief in their own way as they try to support each other without judgment. The hardest part is the "without judgment" part. If someone is not grieving the way you think they should, examine your motives, look at your own grief, and try to refrain from insisting they do it your way. I owe my children a lot for modeling what "healthy grief" looks like without trying to talk me out of the deep sadness I was feeling.

∞

CHAPTER 15

Minimum Daily Requirements

"You chose to walk the earth path, now walk it."
—THE GUIDES

Unfortunately, the first year of mourning, I lost a small fortune trying to hide from the pain, sorrow, and suffering. It is not the way I would recommend to anyone, due to the inevitable financial consequences. While it was not about money, but escape, there were many financial mistakes. I recommend not making any big financial decisions like selling property, gambling, or overzealous shopping, or donations, all of which are diversions to give us a sense of control, numbness, or even short lived comfort.

I stayed a week at a strategically chosen casino on the Mississippi Gulf coast the first Christmas season. Hurricane Katrina had rendered the entire area grief stricken a year earlier. The ride along the coast highway was shocking. There was only sand and dirt where homes, hotels, and restaurants once were filled with vacationers, employed citizens, and laughter. The loss of their loved ones, their homes, and their way of life made the people and workers at the casino an attractive group to share a less than happy holiday. Money was of no concern when trying to suffocate the pain. It was great to be around people who did not know me, to be hypnotized by the machines and lights, to play cards for hours just because I could. All mind numbing, very expensive, activities providing temporary relief.

A common tendency in the grieving process is to isolate yourself from others. While in moderation, isolation may be helpful for you, it is not helpful in financial matters. Use your friends or family as support during these times.

The minimum daily requirement of bill paying, balancing the check book, and other obligations to keep the lights on were more than I could do. I have always been a law abiding taxpayer. However, my 2006 filing was delayed for two years due to my inability to gather the information. Everything reminded me of life before and after July 23.

Because I saw myself as a successful business person, I had a difficult time discussing my financial issues with anyone. It brought up so much shame for me. I finally asked for help from my friend Melinda, who spent a day helping me get organized despite my tears. She explained how it met her need to reach out to support me in a way that was most appropriate.

Look around to see what makes you feel helpless, overwhelmed with sadness, or something you just do not want to do. Chances are pretty good your friends and family are waiting for your request.

Joe, my CPA, remembered that he was my friend before becoming my accountant. While advising me of penalties, he still seemingly without judgment allowed me the time to deal with my finances when I was psychologically ready.

I will always be grateful to them for allowing me to confess my financial transgressions without the anticipated look of horror I expected to see on their faces. We can spend a lot of energy avoiding responsibilities. I discovered the freedom that sharing a burden provides. Pent up misplaced energy is transformed to be used for healing and healthy life affirming growth. My ability to meet the minimum daily requirements returned when I learned to choose life by taking action to manage my grief.

Grief will show you things about yourself that you may have never faced before, like my shame about managing my finances. Forcing me to reach out for help provided an opportunity for me to live more authentically. It enhanced my ability to live in the present moment and see things as they are. If we can't acknowledge something, we can't heal it. There are consequences I am not willing to pay for ignoring my fiduciary responsibilities. Grief provided the necessary wake up call.

Despite its disappointments, pain, and sorrows, life also offers blessings, loving relationships and joyful opportunity. Experience all life has to offer in honor of your loved ones. Seems to me they appreciate it.

∞

CHAPTER 16

Holding the High Watch

*"There is a universal intelligence that we call
God or Soul or Spirit or Consciousness,
and it is everywhere and in all things."*
—WAYNE DYER

Remembering the truth about death and opening to the possibility of continued communication seems to be one of the most comforting things I can do to help myself and others with the pain of loss. We are fortunate if we have friends and family who are comfortable with this communication. Their support, even when they don't know enough about it, is so important.

Maybe you know someone who can help deliver the messages; if not, you can contact one of the recommended resources. As you will discover, there will be many opportunities to acknowledge the continuation of life through nature and other spoken messages from people on this side of "the veil" as well as those on the other side.

You may remember a time when a loved one somehow communicated to you after their physical death. May you find your own way to get to know your loved one. You can access the most loving feeling you will ever know. Whether blessed by friends who support you, or walking this path alone, know that when someone is trying to get your attention it is done with love.

The more you read and learn about life, the less you fear. Essentially, it is true that you are never alone.

Our Holy Helpers on the other side connect in the way that works for you. If not through nature or physical signs, it may be through your sense of hearing, seeing, or feeling. Consider each style to determine what may be yours.

Some people are clairsentient, or clear feeling. This is that intuitive part of you that just knows, senses, and feels something. People who get messages like this use language that reflects the origin. They may say, "I feel like that person is afraid" or "I have a funny feeling." Notice if you use that language.

Some are clairaudient or clear hearing. This is not usually a conversation like you hear in the physical world. It is more telepathically transmitted. No spoken words are necessary, yet thoughts are transmitted instantly. Easier to discern is the language about hearing. The recipient hears in the voice attributed to the person on the other side. It's usually precise, "I heard someone say..." or they may be sensitive to everyday sounds in our world.

Still others are clairvoyant or clear seeing. Difficult to describe, is seeing beyond the physical eye that can be done with eyes open or closed. When I have experienced seeing, it has been more of an elusive somewhat transparent vision. It sometimes comes in all three ways. Each of these ways of communicating can be developed through intention and practice if you are open to it.

Often the only way to communicate to an active conscious mind is to catch it sleeping. Pay attention to your dreams. Many people have such profound communication in their dream state. If you want to receive communication this way, before falling asleep, say that you want a clear dream, keep a notebook by your bed, and begin to write down anything you remember when you wake up. Even if it's only one word, write it down. It may stimulate a deeper memory. People often share that a dream was so real, they could touch, and talk to their loved one. I believe those visits are from them to be regarded as a loving gift for which we say thanks.

I have met people who seem hopeless because they believe, either through religious, or early teaching by authority figures, that their loved one is in hell, or lying in a box waiting for a "second coming." If this works for you, God bless you, I honor your right to choose. The second coming of Christ happens for me every day I remember that life is eternal. Jesus taught me that although we suffer, die, are buried, we rise again in spirit because we all are part of God.

The suffering is intense for those with these potentially limiting beliefs. When they were willing to be open to communication from their children, I have seen a total change in their physical appearance, and approach to their own lives. Knowing their loved one is truly in a better place provides relief beyond compare.

You may be unable to hear or feel due to intense grief. Remember it's a unique process. I told a mother that her son was playing with his dog. Days later that same mother, attending a grief support gathering, was told her son was with his dog and his Uncle Ellis. The mother confirmed that her brother Ellis had crossed over. That same mother called the next day to say she was waiting on a definitive message that proved it was her son. When she is able, she will hear.

In your everyday physical life people try to get your attention. Sometimes you are preoccupied and miss the message. When grief slams into your world, you might not be able to hear anything. People on both sides of the veil will keep trying until they reach you as long as you are open to a relationship with them. How frustrating might it be for those on the other side when they try to communicate and we are unable or unwilling to listen?

Couples often share that they are disconnected in their grief after losing a child. I pray that parents allow each other to grieve in their unique ways, respecting the process until both are ready to consider a new beginning or reconciliation. Allow one another to "hold the high watch" by stepping into a more resourceful state of consciousness. It helps if one is able to see things from a higher perspective when the other is unable to see for themselves. It can be the tie that binds. Taking turns with that role is valuable when you are able to garner the strength, love and gentleness of spirit to do it. The old saying that we hurt the ones we love when we are in pain is why many relationships do not survive the death of a loved one. It is tragic that when we need each other the most is when we may push the hardest.

Driving in Atlanta, thinking to myself how much I wanted more definitive messages from Phil, I heard him say, "Is anything ever enough for you?" Just like when our loved ones are on this side, we should refrain from trying to get them to do things our way by placing pressure on them in order to control them. Like when they were here, trying to meet our expectations, they probably get awfully frustrated with us when they are trying to comfort us, and it never seems to be enough. The way Phil asked the question about being enough, our expectations must be as counterproductive there as they are here.

Due to their higher vibrational frequency, it takes lots of energy for them to resonate at the rate to contact us. They're doing the best they can. Be gentle with yourself. At your vibrational frequency, you too are doing the best you can.

∞

You may wonder about what happens after suicide. It is my understanding from my spiritual teachers, books I have read and messages from those on the other side, that the limitations and ideas we place on their experience from our limited viewpoint doesn't begin to affect the loving presence they feel with their ever present God. If their souls are tormented after a troubled life, maybe someone like Charles Manson, there is a spiritual triage set up where highly evolved spiritual workers meet them to help them on their individual soul's journey.

In the Jesus story, I am "saved" each time I remember that despite the torture, what people said about him or whether anyone believed it or not, he lived again. His Divinity lives on to prepare a place for us. In the Jesus story, he also says to the social outcasts that day they would share paradise with him. Not that they would burn in a hell. I don't believe in the hell I learned about in church. It's a state of consciousness where I've already been in this lifetime and I do not choose to return. Now that's a visual I can wrap my heart and soul around and live my life more completely, knowing I will be with Phillip again in paradise. Anywhere the love we share is present is paradise. That is powerful information to a mother who's lost a child.

We are all connected and there is a purpose for everything under heaven. There are some things that we may never know until we cross over. At the same time, that doesn't prevent me from considering and accepting what seems right for my growth and peace of mind while on earth.

∞

CHAPTER 17

Bless the Children

*"Pretty much all the honest truth-telling there is
in the world is done by children."*
—OLIVER WENDELL HOLMES

We celebrated Stephanie's son Treg's second birthday a month before Phillip's car accident. We loved the sounds of those two and their deep belly laughs when they played roughly together; we often spent time just watching and listening. It seems unusual that a two year old would have such an acute memory of someone who left them at such an early stage of their life. Speaking with conviction, Treg was comfortably able to talk an inordinate amount about Uncle Phil playing with him on any given day. We did not discourage him, only listened.

One Sunday afternoon, while Vivienne was visiting from New York joining the rest of us for Sunday lunch, I asked Treg if he still plays with Uncle Phil. He replied, "Yes, but he doesn't touch me." A silence fell upon the room as we all considered that possibility.

When he was four, he was riding in the car with his mother when he saw a graveyard. He asked what it was and she told him that's a place where we bury dead people, using Uncle Phil as an example. The next time I went to his house, he met me at the door to inform me that Uncle Phil was buried in the ground. One day while he and I were riding alone he said to me, "I am so sad that Uncle Phil doesn't come to my house anymore to play with me." With a heavy heart, the lump in my throat prevented me from further questioning.

Often times we hear that we must become like children in order to experience the kingdom of God. What exactly does that mean? It could mean that we put aside our assumptions and return to innocence in our openness when learning about our world and each other.

Many children have imaginary playmates. Of course, the adults are the ones who call them imaginary. Perhaps children have a keen awareness of their spiritual gifts and we train them not to believe in them. When Vivienne was in first grade, she returned from school with a true/false quiz. One of the statements was, "All Angels have wings." Vivienne had marked it false and there was the red mark beside it showing it was incorrect. She handed me the paper and said, "I don't know how many angels the teacher has seen but some Angels have wings and some don't have any." She confidently turned and walked upstairs.

Tyler told me one day when he was three, "Mom, when I close my eyes I see red: it's my energy, huh?" I truly do not know where these thoughts came from but these little tykes spoke with such conviction as if they were so sure. I think as parents we get nervous and think others will think our children strange if they say things about paranormal experience so we discourage them from speaking about things that may be real to them.

Moments of deep grief can strike unexpectedly with lessons for healing. My daughter Stephanie and her husband had gone on a cruise and I was caring for the sixteen month old, Drew Phillip, and four year old Treg. It had been a while since I had kept up with two energetic boys yet I looked forward to a special time with them. Their parents had not taken an extended trip before; so on the fourth day, the four year old had enough. He had behaved well but was ready to see his parents.

I lay down beside him in the bed as he began to cry, "I want my Mommy and Daddy." I knew no matter of weeping and wailing would get his parents back to him that night.

Many nights I had laid in bed crying, wanting to hug Phillip and I was unable to be comforted. I was unexpectedly in that place of deep loss where no manner of suffering could change the situation. If I went somewhere that reminded me of a special time with Phillip, it was much more difficult to manage.

Whether you are four or fifty, there is nothing anyone can do to lessen your pain until you are ready to surrender. Treg's crying led to his brother's crying, suddenly creating a situation that was not very helpful in moving through these heartfelt moments.

I had a sudden insight that as long as we were at Treg's house, he expected his parents to be there. While we were out doing other activities or at someone else's house, he seemed fine. I suggested we call his paternal grandmother who lives around the corner and go there to sleep. He agreed to go where there was no expectation of his parents being present and he seemingly surrendered to the circumstance and slept well. The next day I took him to school, we ate dinner out, and minimized trips to his house until his parents returned.

How many times have we, in our grief, tried to remain attached to "the way things were," expectant of things that were impossible, and wailed into our pillows? Changing our environment, letting go of expectations, and developing a new schedule could open the space for comfort, healing, and a more peaceful resolution. Just like I was able to help Treg manage his pain, it would be helpful if we would trust a friend or family member to help us see available options that we are unable to perceive alone. Treg could have easily been so overwrought and angry that he would have been unable to listen. The strength he dug deep inside to garner amidst his longing for things to be different, allowed him to be open to a better, if not perfect plan.

∞

CHAPTER 18

When Silence Really Is Golden

"The most basic and powerful way to connect to another person is to listen. Just listen. Perhaps the most important thing we ever give each other is our attention....
A loving silence often has far more power to heal and to connect than the most well-intentioned words."

—DR. RACHEL NAOMI REMEN

I realize that most people are extremely uncomfortable around a bereaved person. I know in my discomfort I have been known to ramble, nervously saying an inappropriate thing or two. I liken being present during this difficult time, to standing in a fire from which there is no escape. Some friends and family avoid the fire, others stand near the fire, and others jump into the fire with you. All of those postures are understandable considering how uncomfortable we as a society are with physical death. Most of us want to be compassionate however close we can get to the fire.

Having been on the receiving end of many attempts at solace, please indulge me. It feels good to get these down. Here are a few things not to say and some things that worked for comforting me during an impossible time.

Things not to say:

1. "You have to be strong." One mother hugged me and said these words in my ear. I wanted to knock her down and ask if that was strong

enough. How strong is enough? The pain is so intense that to be told I must be anything is incomprehensible.

2. "What can I do for you?" Unfortunately, this question was most disturbing to me. I wanted my son back in front of me so I could touch him. I would ask if they could do that for me. Of course, no one could so we both stood there feeling helpless. I have no idea what to do about anything at this time and certainly can't verbalize with any clarity what I may need.

3. "I know how you feel." At this moment, it is difficult for the grieving person to hear that statement with appreciation. The pain is so intense it is incomprehensible that it can be shared.

4. "At least you have other children." If the loss is a child and there are remaining children please do not say these words. While I am grateful for those children, along with them, I must continue to live in a physical world without the one that's gone.

Words and gestures that may be helpful:

1. "I have such fond memories of your loved one." The most helpful thing for me was when people said, "I have such fond memories of Phillip. I will miss his smile." Any story shared by someone who knew him and remembered an event or special time was the most helpful. Generally, these things made me aware that he made a difference while he was here. It was important for me to know that his life mattered which somehow gave me a small sense of comfort.

2. "Your family is in my prayers." If the bereaved is a spiritual person, telling them that you will pray is helpful and soothing to hear.

3. Try not to make it about your story. One obviously annoyed woman called a few days after the funeral to let me know that she stood in line quite some time. She then asked, "Where were you when I got to the front of the line to see you?" Her self-righteous tone rendered her unable to consider what it took for me to stand in front of my son's

casket. Please do not require an explanation. Just know it has nothing to do with you.

4. "I will deliver food within the next few weeks." You might choose to say something definitive that contributes to the well being of the family without creating one more thing to decide. Although eating is not a priority, there will be a need for food for weeks after everyone has returned to their lives.

5. "Please know that we care."

6. Send an email or written note.

7. Consider making the requested memorable charitable donation.

If you have spoken some less than appropriate words to a grieving person, please know that you are forgiven. Even the woman who suggested I was inappropriate by not being by Phillip's casket has been forgiven. It doesn't mean I plan to have lunch with her though.

Sharing my thoughts and feelings about this difficult issue may help you make better choices when expressing compassion to a bereaved person. If you do not know what to say, say nothing. Lovingly listen, hold a hand, or give a silent hug. The song says, "You say it best, when you say nothing at all."

∞

CHAPTER 19

Effective Management Practices

*"I've learned from experience that the greater part
of our happiness or misery depends on our dispositions
and not on our circumstances."*
—MARTHA WASHINGTON

Each day I discover there are actions I can take to help manage grief in a more effective way. People want to help and may suggest something they think may work. I trust myself to know what seems appropriate for me. As I share, consider exploring where there are areas in your life you might find my suggestions helpful. Maybe you are dealing with stress, health issues, or anything that keeps you from living your best life. Trust yourself to know what's right for you.

Emotional Freedom Technique or EFT requires tapping on acupuncture points in your body to achieve relief from feelings and thoughts that are less than productive. Based on Chinese medicine, instead of using needles you use two fingers to gently tap on these points to move blocked energy and to release helpful chemicals in your brain.

My discovery of this technique came during one of those conversations when someone calls for help and winds up providing help instead. John Detillier, a former business colleague, called to ask me for a job for his daughter. While informing him of the sale of my business, and about losing Phillip, he could tell I was having difficulty breathing. With my permission, he led me through a series of tapping exercises that immediately shifted my mood to a more tolerable level.

John's call was another one of many gifts from a most unexpected source. Our previous association was strictly corporate business. He explained that while still employed in the corporate world, he felt a calling to help in the healing arts. Pursuing his dream, he discovered the Emotional Freedom Technique to be beneficial in helping people overcome hardship. Thankfully, his daughter needed a job; he was led to call me, unknowingly, to minister to his deeper calling, blessing me in a profound way. I believe this work is on the forefront of alternative ways of dealing with life, health, and wellness.

I did not understand the process at the time. In my desperation, I was ready to try it; it worked; and I was relieved. John later taught me some tapping routines which really work to transform my sadness when I remember to use them. Be open to possibility, even if it might seem silly, it may heal you in unexpected ways.

∞

Without a doubt, in South Louisiana we enjoy some of the best tasting food in the world. Many say we live to eat rather than eat to live. It's no secret that our relationship to food, particularly if we can afford to eat what we like, is an emotional rather than life sustaining one.

Whatever your attitude about food, an emotional upheaval after a loss can wreak havoc on your eating habits. You can either eat more food than your body can use or you cannot eat at all. Neither is healthy if you are going to restore your well being.

During my intense grief when I was eating because I could, the scales were moving upward at a rapid pace. Frankly the scales matter less than the way your clothes fit and how well you feel. The tightness of my clothes added to my misery.

Paul McKenna hosted a show on TLC called "I Can Make You Thin®." These simple suggestions, that I couldn't believe were so easy to apply, made a difference in the direction my scale was moving.

Eat consciously; eat what you want: eat as much as you want. As soon as you get the first inkling you are full, stop eating, even if you begin again ten minutes later. If you are unable to eat, being conscious about eating things you like might help. It helped that I already had a working knowledge of tapping. When McKenna suggested a routine for unhealthy emotional eating, I immediately began to use it. Eating just because you "can" is definitely emotional eating. Make no mistake, if you are paying attention to your behavior, you know emotional eating. Whether it's a small piece of chocolate, or another plate of food, emotional pain often exacerbates your need for food. A tapping routine once again got results when I did not think I could change anything. My choice to eat consciously and keep tapping, even if it took numerous times a day, shifted my scales and my unproductive emotions.

Tapping may seem ridiculous to you, but once again, suspend judgment and try it anyway. I'd rather look ridiculous while tapping than insane while throwing myself on the floor in an emotional frenzy. You choose.

∞

The advice to pay conscious attention was advice I could apply to all areas of my life. I wondered if I could begin with food and gently look at other areas of my life where I might be doing things without paying attention. Was I allowing myself to become immersed in sad thoughts and stories of missing Phillip without paying attention to thoughts of love and life evident in my life right now? Was I too far into my sad story and therefore making life more difficult both for myself and for others?

Living consciously forces us to be in the present moment. Loss of a loved one reminds us that we have the moments we are living now. Living consciously requires participation in every moment, paying attention to the sights, sounds, and smells around you now.

Living consciously keeps us from getting lost in wishing things were different and minimizes that crazy "mind chatter." Notice how mind chatter is reinforcing the story you tell yourself about life. It matters not whether the story is true or false, it's the one you make up. Sometimes the story is only my dream of what may have been. While grieving the loss of a dream, we must stay focused on the truth of the now.

I know that sometimes I get caught in the story which can serve to inhibit my ability to determine the things I can actually control. Living consciously allows me to begin to retell the story according to the plans I make for my own life right now.

Whatever the past, this moment is the only point of power where I can manage my grief. Taking three deep breaths, in through my nose, out slowly through my mouth, signals my body that I'm taking a break to center myself in the moment. If I get caught up in wishing things were like they used to be, I take the three breaths, and say my newest mantra, "That was then and this is now."

∞

I am comforted when listening to Phil's friends talk about adventures they shared. One friend takes me to dinner about once a month where we have the kind of talks about life, love, and laughter that Phillip and I shared. If you have an opportunity to extend those invitations, please do it. If on the receiving end, I hope you can suspend your pain long enough to say "Yes" and go out. Talk about your loved one. Isolation is not your friend. After all, you've talked about them endlessly with yourself. It's so helpful to see them through someone else's eyes. You may even cry during these times, but do it anyway. Sharing these times can be a balm for your soul as you help the other person deal with their grief as well. Spending time being authentic about life creates connection which makes our lives, and the life of our loved one, more meaningful.

∞

It was quite some time before I stopped having anxiety attacks where I literally felt as if I could not breathe. My cousin, Carolyn, who has two boys the same ages of mine, called regularly to remind me of her support. I made an agreement that when I had those especially difficult times, I would call her and she would support me through them. Hearing the sound of my hello, she began to gently remind me of Phil's love, my love for him, and my responsibility to stay centered. It was a way to reconnect me to the truth and my willingness to live on. If you have someone that makes the offer "to be there" in this way, take advantage of it. Store their number in speed dial and use it.

∞

Resist the urge to verbally attack someone when you are really angry. Intense grief that twists our thinking, causing our mind-chatter to spin out of control, might trigger an undeserved angry response. My exhaustion sometimes kept my angry thoughts in my head rather than allowing them to jump out of my mouth.

Unfortunately, a friend called when I was less exhausted and more out of control. I told her how much I resented that she did not come to be with me earlier in my loss. Calling her selfish and inconsiderate, I recalled anything she may have ever done to disappoint me. She also had two sons and a demanding successful business. Throughout our friendship, we'd shared tense moments about parenting at all hours of the night.

You may have already figured out that my anger was less at the friend and more at life. I was no longer parenting Phillip or running my business. She symbolized all that once was. This encounter allowed me to observe how I had let something, that would normally only annoy me, become a land mine.

∞

Early in my pain, when I still could not stand the sunshine in my bedroom window or hear the birds in the mornings, a friend convinced me to have a session for healing using ancient Tibetan brass bowls, which are tuned to the emotional centers of our bodies known as chakras.

Our bodies are vibrating atoms so it could make sense that they might need soothing after a traumatic experience. When we are in deep trauma, our energy centers get out of balance, creating chaos in our body. It's that out of control feeling, being exhausted without doing anything physical, when emotional, physical, mental, and spiritual circuits are on overload.

While lying down on a massage table in a room with lit candles, surrounded by seven bowls perfectly tuned to correspond to the seven chakras of my body, the practitioner prayed. He asked God to help me pull all the extraneous energy, scattered out into the Universe, back into my core and find strength to center myself as safely held between heaven and earth. Too tired to resist, I suddenly felt relaxed and for the first time, safe, as I closed my eyes and cleared my mind of all things. As I relaxed into allowing the beautiful sounds from those bowls to restore my inner peace, I guess my circuits became rewired. Once again, I did not have to understand it, only to be blessed by it.

An hour later, when I got up and came out of that room, my physical appearance had actually changed. I looked more peaceful and restored. I repeated this weekly for months. It restored a sense of balance and comfort which enabled me to manage and participate in my life once again in anticipation of the sounds of the birds.

∞

A Reiki Master volunteered to come to my home to use her gifts to help move this energy through my body to a more complete resolution of my grief. I accepted her offer and was delighted when she came and had me participate in a most amazing exercise. As she moved her hands around me without touching my body, she asked that I visualize a box that Phillip might give me as a gift. I was to look into the box and find comfort in its contents. While I do not remember all the contents I do remember seeing a sea shell, knowing how comforting it is to me to hear the waves of the ocean. This in itself was comforting, yet not astounding.

What was astounding was that when I was finished with the visualization, as she moved her hands around my heart, she named some of the contents of the box. I never spoke during the visualization, yet she knew my thoughts. This once again provided the message for me that we are all connected. I relaxed and allowed God's love to flow for healing on a much deeper level than I knew before. I took advantage of this gift for a few more sessions, finding each to be more peaceful and powerful.

A more traditional approach to grief relief is to find a counselor or therapist who speaks your language and resonates with your soul. While I visited a Jungian psychologist for three visits, I did not feel any connection and discontinued. Nothing happens by accident. Since she too had lost a son, maybe those talks were for her. Others had success in finding solutions through visits with their therapist. The connection with others who have endured loss is critical in finding a resource for this soul work. Others are eager to share if you only ask.

∞

Hearing from Phillip so soon after his departure made a difference for me. When you are ready, you can contact any of the recommended resources to help facilitate messages from your loved one. Setting the intention to be open to getting to know your deceased one in a new way opens the door to helping make it possible.

While there may be some less than honorable people doing this work, it's just like any other field, doctors, lawyers, teachers, psychologists, there are some good practitioners and some not so good. Get a referral, contact the person to find out what to expect. Also, just like you wouldn't think of going to a doctor and not expecting to pay, you should not expect to work with these gifted and credible people without intending to pay. I know people willing to spend years in therapy or a fortune on medication who would complain about payment for a reading which might provide just the information and guidance needed to lead a more fulfilling peaceful life. Trust your intuition and discern what is right for you.

∞

As soon as you have the strength, begin physical exercise. Walking is a wonderful way to start. It doesn't matter how long you walk. Start with ten minutes and build up to as long as you like. Physical movement helps move that stuck energy that forms those knots in your body. Knots in your shoulders, arms, legs, back, or neck keep you from relaxing.

I sometimes walk around the beautiful lakes at Louisiana State University. Other times I just walk out my front door and head left or right around the neighborhood. Some like to walk on a treadmill, but I have discovered that being outdoors is important to me. Just walk wherever your feet safely take you. If you are reluctant to do it, start tomorrow morning by getting up a little earlier, put on your most comfortable walking shoes and clothes and head out the door before you've had time to think about it. Do this for a week and see what happens.

Some days, as I walk, I cry and tell Phillip how much I miss him. Other days I have creative thoughts leading to productive projects. Some days I just enjoy the outdoors. I have added an iPod filled with educational lectures, empowering music by Karen Drucker, high energy dance music, a little hip hop and rap, and insightful lectures by great spiritual teachers. Only download songs and stories you really like. I was careful not to include anything sad, consciously choosing only uplifting sounds. If you have favorite CD's already, load them on. Plug up your ears and move your feet. It forces you to breathe deeply and gets the circulation going as well. One place you will not be going is crazy if you start walking now.

If you have a labyrinth near you, it can provide a path to walk as you reflect on your needs. The labyrinth is an ancient tool traced back 4000 years. Most are in the form of a circle with a meandering but purposeful path from the edge to the center and back out again. It may be painted on canvass, designed with stones or any boundary that can create a path. A labyrinth can be found in all religious traditions around the world. The Jewish Kabala, the Hopi Medicine Wheel, and the Tibetan Sand Mandala are all examples. The kind I used was a walking path for reflection and meditation. I was encouraged to pray for release from the things that were not serving my highest and best efforts as I was walking toward the center. In the center, I asked to receive all gifts, insight, and courage to take the right action for myself and others. While walking out, I remembered that I am a child of God and I recounted all the blessings in my life.

∞

In quantum physics so many things are possible that I cannot in this single book begin to explain what I hope is true. The purpose of this writing is to share my journey as a mother who lost (every time I say or write this, I hear my son reminding me that he is definitely not lost) a most precious son in hopes of helping you manage grief. I have found that being connected with others who have lost children or loved ones is most helpful. Most importantly, the connection I discovered with my son so soon after his transition has been the most loving thing God could do to help me. We will all deal with death while on this planet. We can be open to the possibility to lighten our burden or we can be closed and judgmental. Just as I do not know my son's soul's journey, which is between Phillip and God, I certainly would not judge anything you do that works for you.

∞

While attending a luncheon to honor women over seventy years old who have made a difference in our community, I was impressed by the zest for life shown by the eight honorees. It was evident that one honoree was used to taking charge of a situation and making the best of it.

When Ms. Spears' name was announced, she walked to the podium, where she was to stand while being introduced by the person who nominated her. In her exuberance, she seized the microphone and began to speak, sharing her story of a seemingly well lived life of service and her latest project of collecting used cell phones and clothing for the Battered Women's Program.

Ms. Spears introduced her guest table beginning with her deceased son, "May God rest his soul." She was such an inspiration to me. To reconcile her son's absence with the blessings she is still making possible for others, sharing her appreciation for her children in attendance, she was a living affirmation that life continues despite its heartbreaking losses. Her command of the microphone conveyed the courage and confidence required to speak, in front of an audience, these parting words, "As long as you are alive...live." Thank you, Ms. Spears, for continuing to inspire others to seize the moment, share the story, and choose life.

For me the choice is clear. Somewhere in the depths of my eternal soul, I know that an eternal presence whispered Phillip's name, he turned his face toward that loving presence and stepped or maybe flew into another realm of being. No matter how traumatic it appeared to me, he knew it was his journey, he accepted it, and he is so happy it happened. I know this in my deepest cells. No matter how difficult the pain of missing his physical presence, I will always take comfort in this knowledge in my heart. I am not worried about where and how he is. I am only concerned that I continue my life's journey to best reflect what I am here to do. My struggle is not with my own death but with life.

To parents who have lost children, anyone who has lost a loved one, I hope you find comfort in receiving any small message from them. Moments of peace may come to you from many sources. These special moments may be from seeing a bird or butterfly that you feel connected to, or hearing a message spoken to you by another person about something only your loved one could have known, or just sensing a presence. May you find comfort as God speaks to your heart and soul in myriad ways to help you manage your grief. While it's an individual soul journey, hopefully we can join together to live life with passion and purpose in honor of those who are leading the way. Stay aware that life with its sorrow, joy, blessings and challenges continues even when we fly away to discover a new world just for us.

∞

Epilogue

As the sunlight entered through my bedroom window, I awakened to the family of birds singing. I smiled before I opened my eyes, thankful for the peace I feel at this moment. My family is planning a trip to Destin, Florida. Jamie, the amazing stay at home mom with great internet savvy, found the rental property; Stephanie did the math and sent the emails informing each of us how much we owe, along with suggested recipes for new beach drinks. Vivienne has made her airline reservations, while Tyler and I plan to show up with little planning while expecting to have big fun. Phillip's memory is always alive yet has become sweeter and a little less painful as we've taken responsibility for our lives. Sharing a resolve to renew our strength, it seems like we may be stronger than ever before.

During my leisurely morning walk, I notice the new spring blossoms and fragrant honeysuckle in the neighborhood. Walking with a friend, as we turn the corner, down the sidewalk is a group of young men meticulously grooming a lovely landscape. The company is owned by one of Phillip's friends, the workers are more friends who love being outdoors.

There was a time this would have reduced me to shambles. Today I feel Phillip's presence, see the smiles on their faces as I approach and enjoy the lively conversation.

I return home to take care of some business. Turning on the kitchen faucet for a drink, I am unexpectedly showered by the sprayer on the side of my sink. Tyler had come by while I was out and taped down the trigger so it would spray me when I turned the faucet on. Dripping and laughing, I call him to complain. He pretends he can't hear me, saying "It's raining at your house? You say you are wet? Huh? I can't hear you, you have to speak up." I hear laughter in the background from the friends gathered with Tyler. I am sure it is being shared by friends gathered with Phillip even though I do not hear it from that transcendent side we have yet to discover. Today I laugh and choose life.

His Eye Is on the Sparrow

I sing because I'm happy,
I sing because I'm free,
For His eye is on the sparrow,
And I know He watches me.

WRITTEN IN 1905 BY CIVILLA MARTIN
MUSIC BY CHARLES GABRIEL

Acknowledgments

It truly has taken a village to get this book into your hands. A special thanks to my editors Jude Wilson and Ginger Vehaskari at GV Editing Associates. Jo Huey, your Alzheimer's expertise seemed to come in handy when communicating in a way I could hear.

When writing The Free Bird Flies, I traveled between my home in Louisiana and an apartment over Dale Fisher Galleries in Grass Lake, Michigan. Imagine my surprise when I arrived and read the sign at the entrance of the one hundred acre farm "The Eyre of The Eagle." I stayed in the Eagles Nest in the Domain of the Eagle. Dale Fisher, the owner is a legendary aerial photographer who has numerous photographic tributes to the development of architecture and life in Michigan. He also has a passion for teaching children about photography though his non-profit Michigan Center for Photographic Arts mentorship program. Being surrounded by his life's work and creativity inspired my work.

Within twenty four hours of my arrival in Grass Lake, while eating lunch at Missy's Grass Shack, local diner, bar, and village meeting place, I met Cheryl and Bill Laimon. Living within walking distance of the farm, they shared their bountiful vegetable garden and bountiful love becoming forever friends. Their fun, friendship, and food provided a great respite when my heart became too heavy to write.

Angie Epting Morris of Voyages Press, Inc., your professional guidance and encouragement, not to mention a stay at your cabin retreat in Big Canoe in the North Georgia Mountains, is an inspiration to any writer. Thank you to Carter Morris, North Georgia fly fishing guide extraordinaire, for catching and preparing the best fresh smoked trout on the planet. Once again my life is blessed by the friends I've gathered along the way who share my passion for helping others enjoy life even when it includes great loss.

The cover design by Valerie Frayer of Frayer Designs uses an ancient Japanese art form to communicate a timeless message. Valerie, thanks for interrupting your life to help heal mine.

Catherine Coulter, thank you for saying yes to Cheryl's request for help. I can't thank you enough for your advice, your generosity and your unselfish attention. You truly inspired me to write.

Thank you to military families around the world who, despite the fear in your hearts, say goodbye to your loved ones, releasing them to their path, wherever it may lead. I salute their brave spirit and your courage, and pray for the day that peace prevails.

Gratitude beyond words goes to Cheryl Robinson, economic adviser, benefactor, and all around genius. When it comes to living life as it is with enthusiasm, excitement, and expectancy for the wonders that come our way, you are the master. Thanks, Cherri, for reminding me that every day is precious.

Melinda Walsh, your lifetime quest for truth brings to all your relationships such authenticity. The way you listened when I was out of my mind and gently guided me home, was a special gift. Thank you for investing in me when life had little value.

Thank you, Donald Bozeman, for being such a loving presence, allowing me to travel along for miles, listening while I tearfully read aloud this manuscript in its premature state. How difficult that must have been for you. Your brilliant mind leaves little space for a long attention span, yet you endured. Intently listening to the words I had so painfully placed on the page, asking for clarification when appropriate, led me to believe I could indeed help others. Your intuitive and healing gifts are an unrealized gift to others. I love it that you have shown them to me firsthand.

My sincere thanks to all the Holy Helpers both seen and unseen who continue to support me in ways I may never know or realize. May the love in me rise to such a degree, that I might always remember the Spirit within me, to be of service to others living on my planet.

Give the Gift of

The Free Bird Flies
— *Choosing Life After Loss* —
to your friends and colleagues.

CHECK YOUR LEADING BOOKSTORE OR ORDER HERE

OPTION 1: Order online at *www.thefreebirdflies.com*
(Gift certificates available)

OPTION 2: Call in credit card orders to BookMasters at **1-800-247-6553**

OPTION 3: To order by mail, complete the form below and mail with your payment to:

BookMasters
30 Amberwood Parkway
Ashland, Ohio 44805

IMPORTANT NOTE:
Make check payable to:
BookMasters

- -

ORDER FORM

___YES, I want _____ copies of *The Free Bird Flies* at $14.95 each, plus $4.95 shipping per book *(Ohio or Georgia residents add $1.08 sales tax per book.)*

Canadian orders must be accompanied by a postal money order in U.S. funds. Allow 15 days for delivery. Expedite Service is also available at additional charges as determined by delivery address.

___YES, I am interested in having BERT FIFE speak or give a seminar to my company, association, school, or organization. Please send information.

My check or money order for $_____ is enclosed

Please charge my: ❏ Visa ❏ MasterCard ❏ Discover ❏ Amer. Exp.

Card # _____

Name as shown on Card _____

Exp. Date_____ Sec. Code_____ Billing Zip _____

Signature _____

NAME_____ Phone _____

ORGANIZATION or BUSINESS_____

ADDRESS_____

CITY / STATE / ZIP _____

Email ___ _____

Signature _____

www.thefreebirdflies.com

Gift Certificate

One copy of

The Free Bird Flies

Choosing Life After Loss

has been reserved especially for you.

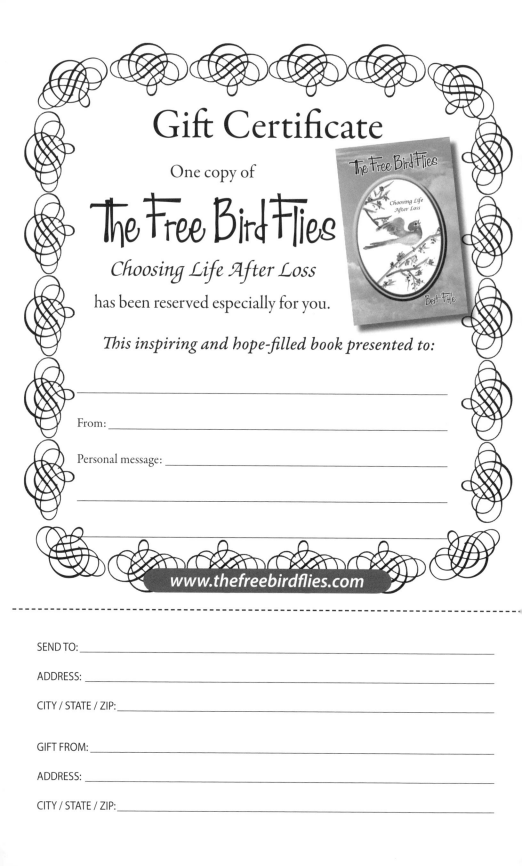

This inspiring and hope-filled book presented to:

_____

From: _____

Personal message: _____

_____

www.thefreebirdflies.com

- -

SEND TO: _____

ADDRESS: _____

CITY / STATE / ZIP: _____

GIFT FROM: _____

ADDRESS: _____

CITY / STATE / ZIP: _____

Resources

Go to *www.thefreebirdflies.com* to find
- People, Places and Things
- Books
- Workshops
- Speaking Engagements

Please visit my blog *Relief4Grief.wordpress.com*. Your willingness to share may allow someone to glimpse a possibility they may not have considered. Together we can heal one heart at a time to honor those who have flown ahead as we decide daily to choose life after loss.

About the Author

BERT FIFE

In July 2006, Bert Fife received the phone call no parent ever wants to get. Her twenty-one-year-old son Phillip had been in a car accident. Despite the doctors' best efforts, Phillip did not survive. He crossed over to the other side that warm summer evening, closing one chapter of the Fife family history while unknowingly opening another. Unsure of how to deal with her grief, Bert relied on her spiritual beliefs, her family and friends, and timely divine messages to show her a new way to look at death—that it's not an ending, but merely a continuation of the soul's journey. Drawing on her background as a professional speaker and life coach, as well as her own grief journey, Bert presents a message of hope to anyone who has lost a child or loved one.